"Fran has creat [barcode] ,ystem for bringing more abundance and prosperity into your life. *The Intentional Millionaire* blends potent spiritual principles with breakthrough strategies and tools that will skyrocket your potential...and your bank account!"
Dr. Stan "Breakthrough" Harris

"If you have the chance to work with Fran you will be inspired but more importantly, you will become about the business of manifesting your million-dollar empire."
Sasha Wilkin

"Thanks to your unwillingness to let me settle, I have not only trimmed my debt significantly but now I also actually have a net worth that's in the black!"
Vince Trebonis

" I wish I could bottle Fran's energy and sell it because I'd make a billion dollars easily."
Gregor Posey

"Even though I wasn't able to sign up for the Millionaires Challenge, you still had a tremendous impact on me. I launched my own TV show..."
Tamm E. Hunt

"...the highest hurdle I had to climb was in my consciousness. Fran helped me to "embrace" being a millionaire and everything changed."
Lars Smith

"I've attended lots of seminars but I have never seen anyone like Fran. Inspiring, authentic and freakin' brilliant. Definitely worth the investment."
Dave Tanner

"Fran's Millionaire coaching and her take on success and prosperity are fresh, different and effective. I feel blessed to have gotten to work with a future billionairess. Go, Fran!"
Kyle Tempe

THANK YOU

I'm excited that you have found and are enjoying one of our products. It is my goal to encourage and inspire people from all over the world to discover the power within them.

I don't believe that I can "empower" anyone. You came to this planet empowered. However, my unique gift lies in helping people to see beyond what they may have believed possible for their lives. It is more than a gift; it's my calling to help you unleash the power "inside" of you. That's what I call inpowerment™!

Leveraging the transformative magic of the written word, audio, video, movies, television, Internet and new media, my goal is to invigorate, challenge and change billions of lives.

I applaud you for investing in yourself and taking one more step toward having the life you not only desire but also so richly deserve.

Peace, passion, power, profits & prosperity!
Fran Harris

The Intentional Millionaire

Winning The Wealth Game With Spirit

Fran Harris

The Intentional Millionaire

Published by InPower University

P.O. Box 3594

Culver City, CA 90231

Tel. 310.590.7191

info@franharris.com

www.franharris.com

Cover Design: Angi Shearstone

© 2006 Fran Harris

All rights reserved. No part of this book may be reproduced in any form or by any means without permission in writing from the publisher; except for the inclusion of brief quotations in a review.

Library of Congress Cataloging-in-Publication Data

1. Money—Psychological aspects.

2. Millionaires – Psychology.

3. Rich people—Psychology.

4. Wealth– Psychological aspects.

5. Succeed in business– Psychological aspects.

ISBN 1-59971-299-7

This book is dedicated to my family.

You know who you are.

I love you all.

Acknowledgments

I am always in gratitude to God, the One, the Divine that blesses all that I am and all that I will become.

Getting a book to market is never a small feat and the reality is that it takes a small army to make it happen. Many people shared their insights, resources and thoughts to help me complete this project and since it's impossible to list everyone, I've chosen to leave out no one.

Thank you ALL for your continued support in everything that I do and aspire to do.

A special thanks to my 100 Women Millionaires Challenge students as well as my coaching clients who inspire me with their courage 365/24/7.

Get Real.

Get Serious.

Get Committed.

Get Rich.

Table of Contents

Intentional Millionaires Daily Affirmation

Today I declare that everything I need to
become more of who I already am is within me.
I release this powerful declaration into the universe,
peacefully having faith that what I intend for my life, is
already happening.

And so it is.

Intention. Spirit. Energy. Actualize.

Manifest.

From The Publisher

The Intentional Millionaire is adding something new and different to current conversations about wealth, prosperity and financial freedom. In this provocative book, Fran Harris boldly proclaims, "We are all born millionaires but only about 1% of us will ever bring this basic spiritual truth into physical reality."

Using a powerful combination of hard knocks experience, engaging tools and common sense, Harris shows you how to identify your unique millionaire path with clarity, spiritual vigor and enthusiasm.

The Intentional Millionaire is broken down into two sections. Part One, "Wealth Training Camp", is all about your money imprints. Harris takes all of the mystery out of how you arrived at your current financial situation and prepares you for a life of unlimited wealth and prosperity.

Part Two, "The Wealth Playbook" provides the tools, insights, resources and exercises to take you to the next level. You'll be introduced to Fran's InPowermentals™, Millionaire Manifesto Moments, and much more!

So, if you're ready to create unimaginable abundance by leveraging spiritual principles and everyday wisdom, grab a highlighter and a comfy chair and let the Wealth Games begin!

The Tao of the Fan

Picture yourself sitting on the floor in the center of a room. Any room. Now imagine that there are hundreds, maybe thousands of one, five, twenty, fifty and one hundred dollar bills flying around above your head.

It's almost as if an industrial sized fan is keeping them circulating. Now imagine that you start to concentrate, I mean really focus on attracting certain bill denominations.

Let's say that you want more fifty and one hundred-dollar bills to show up. All of a sudden you start to notice that the one-dollar bills are flying higher above and the fifty and one hundred dollar bills are within your reach.

You don't have to stand, you don't have to stretch, you just have to reach out and grab them. That's how close they are. Imagine that. Take a moment to truly digest what just happened. See it. Feel it. Be it. That's called intention.

But that's only the beginning. Read on.

Why I Wrote This Book...
and Why You Should Read It

I'm warning you. I am going to say some things in the next hundred or so pages that you have never heard. I am going to say some things that will make you ask, "Is she crazy?" I'm even going to utter words that will blow your hair back and cause you to question the way you've lived your life and spent your hard earned cash.

But most importantly I'm going to delve deep into your relationship with money because it is one of the most intimate and profound relationships we will ever have, yet it's also one of the most "ignored" relationships in existence.

Having said all of the above, my primary goals for writing this book are actually varied: (1) to help bring you into more of a oneness with your money,

(2) to help you create a constant flow of prosperity in all areas of your life and (3) to remind you of the power of intention.

Whenever I write a book, I'm usually asked the same question, "What inspired you to write this book?" It's a great question and there are many reasons people – including myself – write books. Sometimes it's about filling a hole in the marketplace. Sometimes it's about sharing a personal odyssey. Sometimes it's a combination of them both.

Some people say that 'we teach what we need to learn' but I believe that we teach what we are *committed* to learning. So, in a sense, I am simply expanding as I help you expand. We all learn in the same classroom.

Therefore, I invite you to share the lessons in this book with everyone you know because it is only through constant exposure to new information (or old information that hasn't yet sunken in) that we can truly grow and develop in all areas of our lives.

There are many books on the market aimed at teaching you how to "become" a millionaire. Most of these books contain outstanding information that can assist you in amassing fortune and wealth. But I believe there's a huge fallacy in many of these books – they presume that you are not already a millionaire.

The focus in the bulk of many books on the market is on achieving wealth from with-out. The Intentional Millionaire is about actualizing abundance, wealth and prosperity from with-in.

To know the road ahead, ask those coming back.
Chinese proverb

On a more personal note, I wrote this book because one day 10 years ago, I woke up. One day I simply came out of the fog that I'd been in for most of my working life. I was on a spiritual path but I didn't realize the interconnectedness of all areas of my life. Had no clue that my money was simply a reflection of the energy in other areas of my life. I've never really thought about attracting wealth although I was actually quite good at bringing money into my life.

Still, I had no clue as to how it had gotten there beyond the fact that I'd gone to the bank to fill out a deposit slip. Basically I was asleep when it came to my money. I was hardly living paycheck to paycheck but when it came to understanding the energy of money, I was, well, snoozing.

I'd never really stopped to consider that money was actually spiritual currency.

The depth of my financial lethargy became glaringly apparent when I got my first big book advance. At the time I was working for a Fortune 100 consumer products company. I had an enviable compensation package, a company car, expense account, no debt and a comfortable lifestyle. On top of all of this, I was healthy and single with no children. My life was pretty much a cabaret.

In addition to my "job", I was also working as a freelance broadcaster for ESPN, which added a nice chunk of change to my annual income. Life was great. But as I said, it wasn't until a publisher wrote me a high five-figure check that I realized I was in a financial coma.

Yes, it's possible to be financially stable, to have lots of money and still be in a financial coma. Some of you reading this right now are brain dead when it comes to your money and you don't even know it! Don't worry; by the time you're done with this book, you'll be back in the land of the living!

As I said, when I got the first half of my advance from my literary agent I couldn't believe my eyes. I'd never seen a check for that much money with my name on it. I was so thrilled that I took it to Kinko's to photocopy it. I still have that copy somewhere in my garage.

The ink wasn't dry on the back of the check before I was making a list of all the things I was going to "buy" with the first half of my advance. This must be what the "rich" feel like everyday, I thought. *This is incredible!*

You see, the way most publishing contracts work is that you get 50% of the monies upon signing the book contract and the other 50% when you turn in an acceptable manuscript. My plan was to deal with the other half of my "twin" advance check later. It was time to spend, spend, spend and then spend some more. And that's exactly what I did.

You would think that the first order of business might have been to take care of my debt but I didn't have any. Save for a rainy day? I don't believe in rainy days. Put some away for retirement? Nope, didn't believe in that either. One by one, I dismissed all of the "wealth healthy" intuition inside of my heart and being.

Sure, I'd read all of the bestselling books by the financial and wealth gurus of the time. I'd attended (and even said a few amens) at a multitude of self-help seminars. Then after about three days, I silenced all of the would-be mental detractors floating around in my head and it was time to get down to work.

First order of business? A set of custom designed golf clubs. Sweet, huh? But I didn't stop there. I also bought a set for a friend of mine, who was also an avid golfer. Golf clubs for the whole neighborhood, was my motto.

I secured office space in one of the swankiest areas near downtown Austin, Texas and promptly decked out my office with high-end designer furniture. Bought a new car. Plunked down way too much money for a timeshare in Tahoe. And so forth and so on. I was on a roll. I even funded a trip for me and my friends to Las Vegas. I was like a fish in water! I was having big fun and loving my life. Sound familiar to anyone?

After the first half of my advance check was gone, I didn't slow down. I continued to make money in my corporate job. Continued to get broadcasting gigs. Continued to attract deals. And of course, continued to spend, spend, spend and snore, snore, snore through life when it came to my finances.

But it gets better (or worse). Within eight weeks of receiving the first advance check, I wrote the book. Yes, in record time! I was trying to get to that next check! After all, there were cruises, malls and at least 13 states that I hadn't visited.

I'd heard such wonderful things about the Eastern Seaboard. I needed to see what all of the fuss was about for myself. Boy, the second half of that advance couldn't arrive soon enough for me.

Sure enough, the mail finally arrived and again I was off to the races. I was going buck wild. Looking back I could've easily changed my name to Spenderella. It would've been perfect. Within less than a month I had every possible material possession I could want but it still wasn't enough.

There was more damage to do and I was convinced that I was the one to do it. I got busy writing my next book proposal since I had a two-book deal with the publisher. Soon after I turned in the book proposal, I got another sizeable advance. You guessed it, I continued to spend like there was no tomorrow. Zzzzzzzz. Zzzzzzz. I was asleep at the wheel, people.

Then something really strange but oddly predictable, happened. I stopped liking my corporate job. And I don't mean just stopped liking it, I mean I started dreading it. It was still a dynamic and interesting place to work, I suppose. It just wasn't the right place for me. Not any longer.

Now I was really in a pickle. How was I going to leave my job and still maintain the lifestyle I'd grown accustomed to? I certainly wasn't willing to stop traveling or give up the lifestyle I'd grown accustomed to, but clearly something had to give.

By this time I had graduate school student loans, a car note, a mortgage and a host of other undesirable debt. It was time to wake up and smell the tall half-caf cup of coffee. So that's what I did. Which brings us to today.

I learned something through that experience that I believe you should know. If you aren't awake you'll find yourself in situations that are not aligned with who you are or where you want to go! I also learned that if you sleep through the "big" financial moments that come along, you'll miss the opportunity to maximize the blessings that come along with those moments.

Let me explain. Ten years ago I knew that I wanted to be an international speaker, trainer and television personality. I could have used some of my advance money to position myself in the media for the platform I was building.

I could have used some of the money to finance a national speaking tour. I can think of at least 10 things that would have moved me closer to my ultimate goal. Things that were certainly more important than my tailor made golf clubs! Fore!

Clearly the "advance check" story was essential to building the foundation on which I now manage my finances, so it's a positive part of my history; something I use as a stepping stone rather than a stumbling block. But I also learned something else that I believe is equally important for you: the distance between where you are today and where you <u>want</u> to be is a much shorter drive than you think. It truly is. The Intentional Millionaire was conceived to provide you with the simplest, most effective roadmap to fast track your million-dollar empire into reality. Physical reality.

Remember that visual exercise we did earlier with the money and the fan? That's a powerful metaphor for your life. Everything we want is within arm's reach. When we put our attention and in-tention on it, it appears. You can also use this same analogy to explain why certain circumstances are currently present in your life.

In other words, the people, things and energy swirling closest to you - positive and negative - are there because that is where your intention is directed! If you want to bring more goodness into your life, focus on bringing more goodness into your life! If you want better health, make that a focus. If you want better relationships, become intentional about creating healthier ones.

What is Intentional?

So, first things first. I've already talked a lot about intention. But what is intention? The dictionary defines it as "aim" or "motive". Words with which we all have some level of familiarity. What these definitions lack is the fundamental spiritual essence of intention, which implicitly means "purposeful" or "done on purpose". I'll even add, "done in purpose".

That's why I wanted the title of this book to carry a name that signified a life, a mission of purpose. A title that's closely aligned with our spirituality.

The Intentional Millionaire, then, is more than a book, it is a reminder for us to live in purpose rather than merely on purpose. Make sense? Living in purpose means that you are not separate from your purpose or intention. It is not something that is outside of you, therefore, it never vanishes. Consequently, whatever you want to create in your life, all you have to do is access it from within you and it will manifest in the physical dimension.

You've heard of people who have been healed, healed themselves or turned their financial lives around within short periods of time, right? You may have even asked yourself how they did it. Intention? God? Purpose? Spiritual connectedness? Yes!

What is a Millionaire?

Millionaires have been defined as people who have millions. That's the simplest definition. Yes, according to those who define "millionaire" only in those terms, those millions can be in cash or they can be in assets.

My definition of millionaire is somewhat different. You see, we were all born millionaires. We are all sitting on at least three million dollar ideas. How many times have you seen a product on television and thought, "That was my idea" or "I thought of that five years ago"? We've all said something like this at one time or another.

We all have genius within us that if we ever decide to access, will result in the manifestation and actualization of millions of dollars. Unfortunately, some of us will never "see" those millions for a variety of reasons yet they are still inside of us.

Sadly, I believe that the place that holds the largest cumulative net worth – both financially and genius – is the cemetery. More people go to their graves with their genius still inside of them. Most people leave the planet having reached only a tiny fraction of their full potential.

Now, to be clear, I'm not simply speaking in financial terms here. You see, that's what makes The Intentional Millionaire a different kind of book. Yes, I'm going to show you how to access your very own million-dollar empire but it's more important that you understand that money is simply an extension of your energy in other areas of your life. Get the spiritual energy in the right place and the money will show itself. It's already there.

In essence, you are already a millionaire. It doesn't matter how much money your bank statement reveals. You are still a millionaire. And the only reason you might not believe it is because of something I'm going to talk about in a second called "financial separatism".

For now, I want you to get used to the idea of being a millionaire. So, say it to yourself right now. *I am a millionaire.* Say it again. *I am a millionaire.* How does that feel? Strange? Inauthentic? Awesome? Thrilling?

By the end of this journey with me, you will be well on your way to becoming what I call a Millionaire Manifesto – a person who actualizes his or her brilliance and therefore, is adept at bringing their wealth out of the subconscious realm into the physical plane.

What is Spirit?
An internal life force that guides our every move.

When I was 9 years old there were a lot of things I wanted to do. One week it was soccer. The next week dance. The following week piano. And finally the church choir. My mom had footed the bill for most of my endeavors but on this day she either didn't have the money or she saw an opportunity to teach me a valuable lesson about manifestation.

I never got to ask her about this but it really doesn't matter because the gem I got as a result of her decision, laid the foundation for an exciting entrepreneurial journey.

Mom told me that if I wanted the shiny gold choir robe required to sing in the choir that I'd have to earn the money myself. Huh? Where in the world was I going to get that kind of money? "I'm just a kid," I said, with the saddest puppy eyes I could muster. Unfortunately sad eyes were not my mother's weakness so off I went to my room to figure out how to come up with $110. Later that evening I burst into my Mom's room with an idea.

I needed something that I was certain would rake in the cash. There was a lady who lived across the street who had started baking these huge cookies for sale. The kids loved them.

So, I thought, "What do kids love more than cookies?" There was an ice cream truck that drove through our neighborhood once a day and whenever we'd hear his music in the distance all the kids would sprint home to beg for money to buy something. That was it. Kids loved sugar.

Summers in Dallas were brutal. Someone had once sold lemonade and Kool-Aid on the corner but those were drinks that we all could make in our own kitchens. I had to come up with something that kids would like and buy from sun up to sun down. I had it. Snow Cones. It was a stroke of genius, if I say so myself. Now, I can't take all the credit because I did do some brainstorming with my mom but ultimately I would be responsible for about 70% of the operation.

Within a few days we had the cooler, ice, flavorings and supplies. All I had to do was tell the five or six kids on my street about the business and the word would get out. And that's exactly what happened. Within weeks I was making hundreds of dollars, selling a single flavored snow cone for 25 cents and multiple flavors for 50 cents and up.

It was incredible fun and more importantly, it taught me at an early age that anything is possible with a good plan, a positive attitude and a coach who's committed to your success. It also encouraged me to always look inside myself for the answer to any question or problem. By the end of the summer, I'd made over $1,500. That's a lot of snow cones, people!

MILLIONAIRE MANIFESTO MANTRA
I am a millionaire by birth.

Does saying it aloud make it so? No! Saying it only reinforces it. It doesn't create it. It's already truth. That's right. When you were born, you were born a millionaire. Your charge is to take this basic spiritual truth and turn it into a financial truth.

The fact of the matter is that we all came to this planet with everything we need to create everything we want. That means that you are already rich or wealthy beyond your wildest imagination even if you only have $15 bucks to your name.

So, you may be asking yourself right now, "If I'm so rich, why am I so poor"? Good question. The answer is simple:

because you have set your intention to be poor. Plain and simple. If you're one of those people who subscribes to the thinking that "If God wanted you to be rich, you would've been born into riches", you're subscribing to spiritual thought that doesn't serve your highest good.

Those are the kinds of myths that The Intentional Millionaire is will dispel. This book seeks to introduce you to spiritual truths that will release you from the bondage of limited thinking, limited wealth and limited possibility. The truth shall set you free. In this case, financially free!

What is Actualizing?
To bring what already is, into reality.

How The Media Portray The Wealthy

Think of all the images you see of rich people. Donald Trump. Oprah Winfrey. Bill Gates. Warren Buffet. Martha Stewart. The Google guys. Michael Dell. All Millionaire Manifestos who used their talents and work ethic to build billion dollar enterprises. The media does everything in its power to build a gulf between them and everyone else.

True, financially they may be worlds apart from the majority of the world but the reality is that you possess many of the same qualities that these individuals possess, which means that what they've manifested is open game for anyone with the tenacity and intention to go for it.

Think of your favorite Millionaire Manifesto. What do you like most about him or her? What is it about their journey that warrants your admiration? I'm willing to bet that it has NOTHING to do with their money!

You see, the reason I admire folks like Michael Dell is because he had foresight. He could see beyond what was right in front of him. He was just a curly headed kid tinkering around in his dorm room at The University of Texas at Austin. A kid who knew in his gut that he was 'on to something'.

He didn't have the gift of prophecy. He had the courage to follow his dreams. And that's what you have to decide today. Do you have the guts to follow your dreams? Do you have the passion to bring your million-dollar empire into existence?

What Is Financial Separatism?

I've been studying the habits of the wealthy for over 20 years. I started my first business when I was only 9 years old. My oldest brother bought me a subscription to Black Enterprise Magazine, which means that I began reading about successful businesspeople before I truly knew what business was all about.

**It's not possible for you to fail...
it's only possible for you to QUIT**

As an adolescent I would listen to the way people talked about "millionaires". They spoke of them in ways that made them seem untouchable or somehow different than the rest of the world. This was odd to me.

I was still a teenager so I didn't quite understand the whole notion of "separation" and what it meant but I could tell that the general population spoke of, treated and positioned people with "financial means" much differently than they did people with considerably less financial means.

I also noticed that the Millionaire Manifesto spoke of themselves as though they were different than the rest of the population as well. It was fascinating.

The older I got the more I realized that it is, in this case, financial separatism – the idea that somehow because one person has money and another does not – that they are worlds apart. More importantly, this perceived separatism is equally dangerous for both sides – the haves and have-nots.

Let me explain. If I have $1,500 in the bank and I believe that I am somehow not as valuable or valued as the person with $1.5 million dollars in the bank, then I begin to clog up my Blessings Canal with what is nothing more than an illusion based on rubbish I've heard from the media, friends, family and other external voices. These illusions become pictures of what I believe can and cannot become. They are nothing more than pictures and images. They are not real. They only become large and lifelike because we feed them and breathe life into them.

One final note about financial separatism. It is created by both sides of the issue. Some of the people with money start to see themselves as separate from those without and those without start to see themselves through a different lens as well.

The problem with separatism is that first, it's an illusion and second, it creates a dynamic that asserts that one group is better than the other, which in this case if you're not careful can discourage budding Manifestos from striving to reach their own financial potential.

Let's find out where you are on the topic. Have you ever felt that you were more or less than a person with or without a substantial financial profile? Ever thought that your bank account made you an MVC – most valuable citizen – or an LVC – least valuable citizen?

Write The Check

I want you to take out a personal check right now. Write your name in the "payable to" field. Now write an amount of money that you are committed to attracting to your bank account. The amount has to be larger than $1 million dollars. Fill in the date and sign it. One day you will cash that check.

If you don't have a personal checking account, take out a sheet of paper and at the top write "Promissory Note". Then draw a diagram that resembles a personal check. Fill it in with the information from above and you've got the same commitment as the person with the actual check. When you finally get your checking account, make out a check to yourself in the amount on your promissory note.

Movie star Jim Carrey tells the story of how when he and his family were struggling financially and living in a

Volkswagen van that he continued to focus on making it as a comic.

Once he broke into acting and his career started to take off, he wrote himself a $20,000,000 dollar check. He carried this check around with him believing that one day he would be able to cash it. When he signed on to star in the film *The Cable Guy* for a cool $20 million dollars, it was reportedly the biggest payday for a comedic actor. Now that was some serious intention!

MILLIONAIRE MANIFESTO MOMENT

What amount did you write on your check or p-note?

I want you to look at your check. How does it feel to hold a check with that number on it? Check in with yourself and try to get in touch with the feelings you're having as you look at that number. Is it excitement? Disbelief? Doubt?

Fear? Write your experience in the space below or in your journal.

_____

_____

_____

_____

_____

After you've completed the exercise, place the check in your wallet and keep it with you at all times. Look at it at least three times a day, each time affirming silently that one day you will cash it.

This is very important. I call this process Visual Imprinting. There's verbal imprinting and there's visual imprinting. Through a visual imprint you are able to send powerful waves to your subconscious. This, along with the massive verbal imprints you'll engage in, will result in an accelerated million-dollar payday. Trust it. It works.

MILLIONAIRE MYTH

Millionaires fail at a lot of things before they succeed.

MILLIONAIRE TRUTH

Millionaires TRY a lot of things and ultimately succeed.

When I was a college athlete I would lay in my dorm bed visualizing playing a spectacular basketball game. In my movie I would shoot extremely high percentages from the floor.

Get to the free throw line all night and dazzle the fans with my acrobatic dives on the floor for loose balls. The funny thing is that whenever I'd engage in these exercises I'd almost always have incredible performances!

So if you're one of those people who thinks affirmations and visualization are too "cushy feely", let me assure you that you are missing out on a powerful tool for actualizing and manifesting.

Visualization Exercise

Think about where you want to be this time next year. I want you to write it down in vivid details. What will you be doing for a living? Where will you live? What will your days be filled with? How much money will you be making? How will you be serving the world? Write it all down.

_____

_____

_____

_____

_____

_____

_____

_____

_____

_____

_____

RECEIVING EXERCISE

How much are you worth a month? If you were in the career of your dreams, how much would you make each month? I want you to double that amount.

Now envision someone bringing you that amount of money in cash and placing it in your lap. Tell me what happens for you when you visualize being given what you're worth each month.

Write down how you feel as you receive this money. Go ahead and use the space below to capture what's going on with you right now.

_____

_____

_____

_____

The Great Love Affair

I'm willing to bet that you've never thought about being in an intimate relationship with your money. Am I right? For many people this is the primary reason that they haven't been able to manifest their millions. You're in good fortune today because I'm going to show you how to have a torrid love affair with your money and how doing so will bring more of it into your life.

Take out a bill or coin. I want you to hold it in your hand, look at it and say the following: _I love you. I appreciate you and I see you multiplying beyond my imagination._

Now, you may be asking yourself the same question Tina Turner asked in her mega hit song: what's love got to do with it? When it comes to anything you want to expand, love has everything to do with it.

By showing your love and appreciation for your money, you communicate positive vibes that nurture its growth and explosion. Remember, what you feed, grows. If you feed your money cues about lack and scarcity, that is precisely what will show up for you. If you are loving and respectful of your money, more of it will also show up for you.

If I'm So Rich Why Am I So Poor?

What a great question. There are a couple of reasons you may be struggling financially, all of which have to do with either your consciousness, your habits or a few factors in between – which we'll get into shortly.

If you are experiencing financial hiccups it's probably due to the fact that you have not yet discovered a way to bring money into your life on a consistent, viral basis. That's why there are poor and rich people in the world.

MILLIONAIRE MYTH

Rich people work longer than other people.

MILLIONAIRE TRUTH

Rich people work smarter than other people.

Am I saying that poor people want to be poor? No, they don't *want* to be poor, they *intend* to be poor! Let me explain. We are all born into certain circumstances. Some of us are born with silver spoons in our mouths, some of us are born with nothing in our mouths.

The point is that while we may have nothing to say about how we enter the world, we have everything to say about how we leave it. In other words, the sum total of your life today is a result of the choices you've made. You are where you are today because of conscious or subconscious choices.

You've heard it a thousand times but maybe you haven't really considered it truth for you. So, let me say it again. You are where you are today because of the choices you've made. The house you live in, the car you drive, the relationship you're in, the color of your toothbrush and the color of the shirt you're wearing right now — all a result of the choices you've made. You could also be struggling because there are lessons you need to learn that you are resistant to learning!

If we keep the conversation financial, your current portfolio is a mirror of your choices, which means that you have the power to change your reality in an instant by simply changing your choices. Not tomorrow but in this instant.

As you read this sentence there are people in the world who are changing their circumstances. They are changing their consciousness, their mindsets and their behaviors. As a result their realities are changing.

We've heard it too many times: do what you've done in the past and you'll get what you've gotten in the past, plain and simple. Want something different? Do something different. It's really that simple.

If you don't believe me, go to your local bookstore and read biographies of wealthy individuals. Here's what you'll find. Chronicle after chronicle of how people escaped poverty, eluded illness and disease, and in many cases risked their lives to create the existence they wanted.

Even today people are sneaking out of their homelands in search of a better life for themselves and their loved ones. It happens all the time. These individuals are not waiting on someone to give them permission to claim their riches.

Something within them affirms that they were born with the right to pursue their dreams. You too, have the same right.

You came to this planet with everything you need to create everything you want.

So, if it were that easy, wouldn't everyone be rich? Nope. Because financial freedom is not only the result of desire, it's the result of intention. I was not born into a rich family. My parents were working class people who taught me that entrepreneurship is not only a necessity but also a requirement for building the life I want.

While I could have decided that the society we live in is not an optimal place for little black girls to thrive, I chose to see it as a place where I could become whatever I chose. Notice I didn't say 'whatever I wanted' but rather whatever I chose.

You see, everyone *wants* to have an MBA, a mega bank account, but statistics show that only a small percentage of the human population will.

A few weekends ago I spoke at national network marketing convention. The room was full of over 500 eager, hungry network marketers who were on fire about a new product. I asked a simple question. One that we've heard many times before. "How many of you are ready to become multi-millionaires?"

The room erupted with applause. Then I posed a second, more important question. "How many of you are willing and committed to bringing that simple truth into reality?" Again applause. But here's the rub. Everyone in that room – all 500 individuals – can manifest millions upon millions of dollars but only about 1% will. That means that about 5 out of those 500 people will actually "see" their millions in their lifetime.

Now, do they all want it? Of course they do. Who doesn't want financial freedom? But will they all experience it? Absolutely not.

If that is the sobering truth, why am I writing a book about it? Because I want to change those odds. I want more than 1% of the population to experience the joy of financial freedom. Each time you take a tiny step toward uncovering secrets of wealth, success and actualization, you take a giant step toward realizing your full potential as a human and spiritual being.

So, no matter where you are today, you can still expand. No matter how deep in debt you are, you can still rise. This book is as much for the person who has $12,000,000 in the bank as it is for the person who has $3.44 in their cookie jar. The Intentional Millionaire is not about money.

It's about the spirit of actualizing wealth. The consciousness of richness. The mentality of becoming financially free. Once you embrace the consciousness, the spirit and the mentality of a millionaire, money will flow through your life like a fountain. Count on it. And most importantly, expect it. Quite simply, the principles in this book are designed to help you become one with expansion.

If you can believe that you and your money are one - and not separate - you will turn your financial life around almost immediately. This I guarantee. In other words, money is nothing more than energy.

You are energy, therefore, you and your money are reflections of one another. The techniques in this book will not only stretch you to become more of who you are, they will also accelerate your ability to bring what you intend into the physical dimension.

It doesn't matter where you came from, which schools you attended, what racial group you identify with or how long you've been on this earth. Your ability to manifest what you want will depend on one thing: your intention.

There are people whose beginnings were far more auspicious than yours or mine who are now leading successful and prosperous lives. These same individuals could have chosen to let their circumstances define them but instead chose to define their circumstances. Take Patrick Ireland for instance.

He was a student at Columbine High School in Littleton, Colorado on the day it was besieged by gunfire on April 20, 1999. On that fateful day he was shot several times including in the head and in the foot yet Patrick did something that is almost unbelievable.

Over the course of three hours he dragged his body from the floor and climbed out of a window to safety. He suffered serious brain damage and to this day, still has a bullet lodged in his brain. Defined by his circumstances? No, Patrick survived the heinous attack on him and his classmates and pulled a 3.8 grade point average during his sophomore year in college. With a bullet lodged in his head! Now, that's defining your circumstances!

The Choice Is Yours

I want you to take a moment to identify a circumstance in your life that you have allowed to define you. It could be something from your recent past or something from a long time ago.

Write it down.

Now, write down why you CHOSE to let it define you.

_____

Next, write down the cost you paid mentally, physically, spiritually, emotionally or financially as a result of your choice.

_____

And finally, write down what you are going to do TODAY to define the circumstance and grow from it.

_____

_____

_____

If you'll notice, I didn't give you a whole lot of space to answer those questions. Do you know why I did that? Because life is very simple. The reasons we do most things are not complex at all. Fear, doubt, intimidation, love, joy, ignorance and so forth and so on.

Many of us allow our circumstances to define us sometimes because we don't know that they don't have to. In other words, many of us don't realize that we have the power within us to change any external or internal truth about us. Instead we marry our wounds and begin a lifetime of nursing them instead of finding a way to heal them.

Your life today = Choices + Repeated Actions

Let's define each of the terms above. A choice is a selection. You chose to brush your teeth today. You chose to drive instead of taking the bus. You chose to buy this book.

A repeated action is something you do on a consistent basis. If brushing your teeth is a repeated action, there's a good chance that you have excellent dental health. If you've chosen to read three books a week there's a good chance that this repeated action has left you with a solid command of language and story. If you've chosen to use cash instead of credit cards, there's a good chance that this repeated action leaves you with little or no credit card debt. And so forth and so on.

You've bought this book because you have a deep desire to create something in your life. You made a choice to buy this book over others and you took an action by actually reading it once you received it. This is the formula for becoming a Millionaire Manifesto. Choices plus repeated actions will almost always get you the results you seek.

Maybe it's money. Maybe it's more money. Maybe it's love, harmony, wellness or laughter. I don't know what you seek but I do know that what you are being exposed to in The Intentional Millionaire has the power to change your life forever...if you are ready to be changed. Are you? Then let the transformation continue!

Millionaires don't live for the moment, they live IN it.

Millionaire Manifestos DARE

As I learn more about attracting wealth and prosperity, I'm narrowing the list of personal qualities of high actualizing individuals each day. I've discovered that Millionaire Manifestos tend to share several traits with four at the forefront. D = Decisive. A = Action Oriented. R = Results-centered. E = Energetic.

Manifestos are decisive.

How many times have you seen a fantastic opportunity, known it was a fantastic opportunity yet were afraid to make a move because you wanted to think it over a little while longer? Now, to be clear, there's value in weighing the pros and cons of a course of action but let's face it, many of us don't really mean, 'I want to sleep on it.' We really mean, "I'm too afraid to say yes in this moment."

That's what we really mean. I believe that most of us are so accustomed to ignoring our intuition that we don't always recognize when a life-changing opportunity is staring us right in the face!

Manifestos are action-oriented.

Once a decision's been made, it's time to sing or pass the microphone to the next person. Too many of us him-haw around. We won't make a decision. And if we make one, we become paralyzed with the enormity of what that decision means for us. If you are to become a Millionaire Manifesto, you must not only be willing to make the tough decisions, you must also be willing to take that next critical step and DO SOMETHING!

Manifestos are risk and results-oriented.

Nothing ventured nothing gained, right? No truer words were ever spoken. Unless we're stretched beyond what we perceive to be our limits, growth is impossible. Manifestos know this better than anyone. Most of us have been to the mountaintop to the valley and back to the top several times over. We have risked everything to realize our dreams. We have gone against the counsel of people we love and respect. We've walked through our fears. We've gone against our better judgment in favor of finding out what that "gut feeling" was about. We've done all of these things because we understand one undeniable truth: nothing ventured, nothing gained.

Do we enjoy the risk? Not always. But we know that the rewards, the results are what keep us going back to the well. We know that the degree to which we are willing to risk is in direct proportion to the degree that we will succeed.

Manifestos are energetic.

When I speak of energy here I'm talking about two different kinds of energy. The first kind of energy is the kind you're probably thinking of. Enthusiastic and passionate? Absolutely! Manifestos are excited about bringing more prosperity into their lives. It's fun! It's thrilling to know that we all have the power to create the lives we want.

That's why if you took away all of the worldly possessions including every single cent from a Millionaire Manifesto, they would be able to rebuild their empires within a reasonably short time. Take everything away from someone who has not yet adopted a millionaire mindset and they would fold up the tent and call it a day.

The second kind of energy is a kinetic frequency on which millionaire manifestos operate. It's an invisible currency that fuels them. Do you have this high level voltage? Absolutely! However, most people don't realize that this power is inside of them...or they're afraid of it.

They're too busy looking for an outside catalyst to jumpstart them. Don't wait to be discovered. Discover yourself! Uncover your millions! They're in there, just waiting on you to awaken the genius within.

You are a magnet. What are you attracting today?

What Is Your Money Doing?

Today, right now, your money is doing one of two things. It's either making you more money or it's draining your current money. Take a deep breath and answer this question. Is my money mostly making me money or is it costing me more money? If you're investing, saving, or buying real estate, then clearly your money's making you money.

If you're living beyond your means, accumulating undesirable debt and refusing to address your relationship with money, it's a sure bet that your money is sucking the life out of your money.

Your Money Imprint

An imprint is a stamp or an impression. We all carry the stamps of those who raised us. To some degree we've all been affected by the imprints of those who influence us – our parents, teachers, spiritual advisors, siblings, and friends, even the media. All of these things play a part in shaping how we see money, how we experience money, how we attract money, how we treat money and how we feel about money.

Let's do a quick imprinting exercise. When you were growing up...

Who cared for you?

Who paid for food?

Who did the grocery shopping?

Who worked?

Who paid the bills?

IMPRINT MEMORY

Recall a moment from your past that you're sure is still dictating how you relate to money in your life today. Use the SPAR system – Scenario, People involved, Actions taken, Results.

Here's an example. When I was growing up whenever money was tight in our house, my mother would randomly blurt out, "Don't ask me for any money!" These outbursts were so random that they actually became comical. It was almost as if she were trying to stop us before we even thought about asking for anything. "Don't ask me for any money!" I can still hear those words echoing in my ears!

This imprinting stayed with me for a full year. I would want to ask my mother for money and would stop myself because I figured she was predisposed to saying no. Years later this imprinting stopped me from inquiring about money in professional settings as well, until one day I realized what was happening. It was like a bell rang in my ear. I broke the pattern and I stopped the effects of my mother's imprinting. On the spot.

Now, let's reframe your situation. Knowing what you know now, how can you respond differently to this imprinting?

MONEY LANGUAGE

In your home, what were the conversations around money like?

List three phrases/statements that you heard a lot in your home?

1.

2.

3.

List three phrases/statements you heard in your church or spiritual community.

1.

2.

3.

Now, I want you to look at your answers. How do you think these realities shaped your current money reality? Can you see why you've made the choices you've made?

Let's go to the next important stage in your money development. Your money values.

Core Values Around Money

What's your general philosophy on having tons of money?

What (or who) do you think shaped this philosophy?

Has this philosophy served you well? How so? If not, explain.

What's your position on borrowing money?

Are there people from whom you wouldn't borrow money? Why or why not?

If a friend wanted to borrow money from you what would be your process for deciding if you'd grant the wish?

What if the friend never repaid the loan, how would this affect your relationship?

How do you feel about credit card debt?

What's your take on maintaining "Good" Credit? And why?

What's a "good credit score "to you?"

Do you sign agreements when there's an exchange of money between you and friends and family? Why or why not?

List two "borrowing" incidences. How were they handled?

List two "loaning" incidences. How were they handled?

Millionaire Manifesto Moment
If I told you that your life depended on your ability to make $10,000 in the next 12 hours, what would be your game plan?

EMOTIONAL INVENTORY

Check all of the emotions you associate with money.

____Acceptance   ____ Amusement   ____ Anger

____Apprehension ____Awe   ____ Bitterness,

____Comfort   ____Confidence,   ____ Depression

____Disappointed ____Embarrassed ____Envy

____Fear   ____Frustration   ____Gratitude

____Grief   ____Guilt   ____Hate

____Happiness   ____Hope   ____Joy

____Jealousy   ____Love   ____Nervousness

____Negativity   ____Pain   ____Peace

____Shame   ____ Terror   ____Unhappiness

____Vulnerability ____Wonderment ____Worry

ICTABAH → ICK-Tah-Buh.

The next diagram takes all of the mystery out of your financial picture. It is a simple yet powerful illustration that reveals why you are where you are today. It goes like this. Your imprints inform your conditioning, which influence your thoughts, which shape your attitudes, which impact your beliefs, which drive your actions, which form your habits, which explain your RESULTS!

ICTABAH → Results

Imprints ⇒ inform

Conditioning ⇒ which influences

Thoughts ⇒ which shape

Attitudes ⇒ which impact

Beliefs ⇒ which drive

Actions ⇒ which form

Habits ⇒ which explain

Your Results!

Let's delve a bit more into the acronym.

Conditioning: the process of molding something or someone into a certain way of thinking.

The imprinting you received early in life is only temporary unless you adopt it as permanent. For example if your parents repeatedly said, "Money doesn't grow on trees", this conditioning might explain the results you've been able to bring about in your own household.

Do you ever find yourself saying the exact things your parents used to say to you when you were growing up? That's the power of conditioning.

Thought: an idea produced by thinking.

Someone once said that we have over a million thoughts a day. That's a lot of thoughts. Consider the fact that there's hardly a moment that goes by when we aren't thinking. That means that you have a substantial number of opportunities to change "the way" you think about your money, therefore, you have a substantial number of opportunities to create a more positive conversation in your head. A more positive conversation on any topic often leads to more positive results in that area. This is just one of many spiritual truths.

Attitude: a way of thinking about something or someone

My fifth grade Language Arts teacher used to say (at least 20 times a day), 'your attitude determines your altitude'. I must admit that I had no idea what Ms. Mulkey was talking about most of the time. She spoke in rhymes quite often and seemed to fill our days with beautiful language that I'm sure she hoped we'd one day appreciate!

As I got older I did finally understand the wisdom in this short quote. She was trying to impress upon us the need to have a proper way of thinking about education and learning. She knew that our perspective on these important issues would influence our ability to become productive, successful young adults. She was right.

Belief: a firm opinion about something

At first glance most of us think 'religion' when we hear the word belief but it truly extends to many other areas of our lives. Our financial beliefs are often tied to the beliefs of our parents, which is why it's so crucial to establish your own value and belief system around money.

Action: the process of exerting energy

If your conviction is that money is the root of all evil, then that belief will influence you to "behave" or "act" in very specific ways, right? You may avoid it, throw it away, give it away or repel it at all costs. This action is in direct correlation to your belief system.

Habit: a consistent tendency

We are the sum total of what we repeatedly do. If you repeatedly eat lots of vegetables, grains and fruits, you'll be more likely to have healthy intestinal and digestive health.

Result: the outcome

What has repeatedly shown up in your life – your result – is in direct proportion to your habits. Healthy habits often lead to healthy results. Unhealthy habits almost always lead to unhealthy and undesirable results.

Here's the good news. You are in 100% control of your ICTABAH. You control the effects of your past imprinting. You control the impact of your conditioning. You control your thoughts by filtering what you read and listen to. You shape your attitudes by what you continue to think about each day.

You control your beliefs by keeping your attitudes in check. You can always choose to act in a certain way, which means that when you look at your life and you see the results you've garnered, the person most responsible for what's on the right side of the equal sign in the equation below is - YOU.

ICTABAH = Results

Review the ICTABAH diagram again. Where has your prosperity pipe gotten clogged lately? Are you giving in to unhealthy habits? Have you allowed your thoughts to stray away from positive, productive and prosperity-filled images? Is there a breakdown between your thoughts and your actions?

Take a moment to review ICTAHAH and become aware of your money consciousness. Make a mental note of what you need to start doing in the next moment to align all of the components of ICTABAH so that you can create the results you want.

"Breaking Through Our Conditioning" Exercise

The most effective route to making change is by examining our imprinting. Remember, an imprint is nothing more than a stamp. It can be changed in the twinkle of an eye.

By now, you're probably asking yourself why we're doing all of this "work"? And the answer's really quite simple. The things that keep people from living abundantly often have little to do with their physical limitations or intellectual aptitude and almost always more to do with their self-imposed mental or spiritual limitations. As I said earlier, get the spiritual energy flowing and everything else will follow. So, let's continue checking out your conditioning.

I was raised to believe that money was

_____

I was raised to believe that rich people were

_____

When my parents discussed money, it always felt like

Whenever I'd ask my mother (or guardian) for money, she would

Whenever I'd ask my father (or guardian) for money, he would

My religious/faith role models talked about money as if it were

Belief Inventory Exercise

Rank yourself from 1 to 5 with regard to each of the following statements.

1 – Strongly Disagree, 5 – Strongly Agree

____ Money's necessary for happiness

____Getting rich is a matter of luck

____Becoming wealthy is about choices

____Wanting to be rich is not spiritual

____I'll probably never be rich

____I don't think people in my (race, gender, etc.) can ever be wealthy

____If I become rich, I'll probably lose it all

The Intentional Millionaire

___Money's the root of all evil

___The love of money is the root of evil

___God doesn't smile on wealthy people

___Greed is inevitable if you have a lot of money

___People who have a lot of money probably got it illegally

___I don't really need a lot of money to be happy

___Money's not that big of a deal

___It's good not to WANT money

___Poor people are more spiritual than rich ones

___I'm too old to become a millionaire

The Intentional Millionaire

___I'm too young to become a millionaire

___Financial security will only come if I stop sinning

___If I had money, I'd give it all to the poor

___Poor people can't help it that they're poor

___You can't really make money unless you're good at math

___Given my history, financial freedom's not in my cards

___Debt is to be expected and accepted

___If money comes easily, it's probably not worthwhile

___I think you should work hard for your money

The Intentional Millionaire

____Wealth is for white males

____All of the million dollar ideas are gone

____Women shouldn't strive to be rich

____Talking about money is bad

____Bragging about how much money you have is bad

____It's getting harder and harder to get rich

____If I had more time, I could make a fortune

____I don't believe you should ask for a raise

____It is better to give than to receive

___If God wanted me to be rich I would have been born wealthy

___Only smart people make money by investing

___I have an underlying resentment toward rich people

Now that you have some ideas about how your past may have affected your present, let's talk about the present.

About seven years ago I wrote a book about raising financially responsible children. I did workshops around the country where parents came and learned how to become better money role models for their kids. What I learned in those seminars opened my eyes to some of the challenges facing adults in today's society.

I discovered that there were several basic profiles of money managers. Let's see if you can find <u>you</u> in one of

these profiles. Remember, the key to becoming a
Millionaire Manifesto starts with knowing thyself. There is
no judgment in any of these descriptions. Like everything
contained in these pages, this exercise is designed to
propel you to new heights rather than knock you down.

THE WALL STREETER

Your checkbook is balanced to the punctuation mark. You
check your account online twice daily. To you money may
mean security. It may feel like the one thing you can
control.

Potential Issues: You're so controlling with money that
it's difficult for money to flow freely. Sure, you may not
have any debt, you may have achieved the elusive perfect
credit score, you may have the recommended 6 months
emergency cushion and the 401K but you're probably also
carrying around a burden in the form of "fear".

Fear of not having any money. Fear of a catastrophe striking. Fear of not being able to provide for your family. This isn't the healthiest atmosphere for money to grow. Yes, you may appear to be in a good place, however, consider how much more money you'd attract if your energy weren't so stifled.

THE GREAT PRETENDER

You've got all the "toys". The luxury car, the house, the jewelry, designer clothes and country club memberships but you could also be struggling to pay your bills each month. It's not a stretch for you to talk about how much money you make, how much you just spent on your vacation or who you had dinner with last weekend at the "club". Appearances are paramount for you.

Potential Issues: A financial breakdown could be lurking around the corner if you don't get real. In your mind it's more important that other people think you have money than it is to truly have it. You are caught in the illusion of money and perceived prestige. A rude awakening is in your future.

SQUEAKERS

I call you Squeakers because if you were to open your wallet right now it would probably creak like a door in a haunted house. You are a tightwad. You never lend money to people. You are thrifty and proud of it. You shop for bargains, rarely buy retail and may even have a physical reaction to buying something at regular price when you discover that it went on sale two days later after your purchase. It wouldn't be out of character for you to return the full-priced item and re-buy it at the sale price!

Potential Issues: Money will have a difficult time breathing in this environment, which means that although you may "think" you are financially stable, your anxiety around money keeps you from manifesting your true potential.

THE MONEY MARTYR

You feel bad if you have too much money so you spend unwisely or give it all away. You may even think that money's bad or that God doesn't want you to have it.

Potential Issues: You will always struggle because to you, it's "good" NOT to have money. You co-create your meager existence. You participate fully in the process of "not" manifesting your millions.

THE MONEY AVOIDER

Your motto is "I don't wanna deal with it" so you don't open your bills and you would rather chew nails than discuss money.

Potential Issues: You create BIGGER obstacles for yourself because you see money as something to avoid. If you want to avoid it, how do you expect it to come into your life?

THE MONEY GRINCH

You have nothing good to say about money or those who have it. You have a basic hate-hate relationship with it. Your disdain is evident in how you use it, how you speak about it and how you respond when others get it. I once heard a comic say that when her neighbors got a new car her father would always remark, "Wonder what they did to get that?"

Potential Issues: You are in direct conflict with manifesting millions. You repel money with your negative energy. Don't worry. Money will steer clear of you!

RECAP

Which one are you? And yes, it's likely that some of you are hybrids or that you have vacillated between several profiles. So, go ahead, get in touch with your type because this is going to reveal your habits. Here's a scenario.

Scenario: If I handed you $1000 in cash what would you do with it?

Wall Streeter

_____

_____

_____

_____

_____

Great Pretender

_____

_____

_____

_____

_____

Squeakers

_____

_____

_____

_____

_____

Money Martyr

_____

_____

_____

_____

_____

Money Avoider

_____

_____

_____

_____

_____

Money Grinch

_____

_____

_____

_____

_____

Now that you know what you'd do in this situation let's discover some strategies you can start implementing to create different financial realities for you. For each type, there are some specific remedies.

Wall Streeters: Try not to balance your checkbook for one day. When you think of money, think of it as plentiful rather than as something that could potentially run out. Close your eyes and picture Niagara Falls with money as the Falls.

GREAT PRETENDERS

Draw a line down the center of a sheet of paper and get real about what you can and cannot afford. Divide your sheet of paper into quadrants and place all of your debt into the appropriate quadrants:

- Undesirable & High Interest Debt(credit cards)
- Delinquent Debt (possibly credit cards, loans, etc.)
- Refinancable Debt (automobiles, homes, etc.)
- Desirable Debt (house, other real estate, etc.)

Now, devise a plan to systematically get your life back into balance. You have some decisions to make. Maybe you need to address paying down some of your undesirable and high interest debt. Or depending on your situation, it may make more sense for you to refinance your car to lower your payments.

The point is to take a realistic look at your current reality to see how you can creatively increase your net worth and your overall financial picture. Finally, realize that you have some internal issues that you've been trying to fix with external bandages.

SQUEAKERS

Get in touch with why you believe that if you don't scratch and save every single penny that you'll end up homeless or penniless. If this is old imprinting from your childhood, choose to create a different reality for yourself. Loosen your grip. Whenever you notice that you're in the "death grip" money mode, relax.

MONEY MARTYRS

Money does not make people evil. Money only makes people more of who they already are. Your action step might include instituting a "no giving money away for 30 days" policy. Make the effort to become aware of which emotions are online when you feel the urge to give your money away. Do you feel guilty for having money? Do you know the difference between appropriate and inappropriate giving?

MONEY AVOIDERS

It's simple. Sit down at the table and open your bills. All of them. Look at your financial picture and you'll probably discover that things are not as bad as they seem. Might be a good idea for you to talk openly about your anxieties. No judgment, just discussion.

MONEY GRINCHES

Take out a sheet of paper and write 50 positive attributes of money. Once you've written them, read them out loud three times. As you're reading them, try to send a different energy into the universe about money. Pay close attention to any physical cues you may have as you read.

Changing The Conversation About Debt

I'm not going to spend a great deal of time on this subject because there are plenty of books out there on the topic, written by people who do a great job of addressing the issue. I do, however, have a few thoughts that warrant your attention.

Debt. Ever wondered why it sounds so much like the word "death"? I have. I don't think it's a coincidence that the two words are so similar. Everywhere you turn someone is telling you how bad debt is. How brutal it is. How deadly it is.

You can't turn on a financial television show or even the 10 o'clock news without someone *shaming* you for having debt. What kind of energy do you think that creates? You guessed it. It clogs your Blessings Canal.

Here's an example of what happens to a lot of people who are on the brink of manifesting millions. You've had a hard day at work. You come home and plop down on the sofa. You turn the television to a financial show where you hear the host ripping the guest up one side and down the other for having $21,000 in credit card debt.

You start thinking about how much credit card debt *you* have and subconsciously you start to feel reprimanded as well. This "you're so awful" message goes to your heart and immediately starts to manufacture all of those words and phrases you know so well. *I'm never going to get out of debt. Credit card debt will kill you. The rich don't have debt.* And so forth and so on. You were feeling pretty good about yourself when you got home but now you're kind of depressed. You muddle through a meal, hit the showers and go to bed.

The last image emblazoned on your mind is the television host wagging his finger in the guest's face, reminding her that it's going to take 12 years to get out of debt. You eventually fall asleep but when the alarm clock sounds at 5:30, guess what's your first thought? Yep. I'm such a bad person for having credit card debt. And instead of feeling inspired to take action, you figure why try. Ever felt that way?

So, here comes one of those statements that is going to shock you. Brace yourself. Here goes. Debt, in and of itself is not death. In fact, credit cards have as many virtues as pitfalls.

The reason people keep force-feeding us all of this propaganda about debt is to create fear. And it's worked. You can hardly talk to someone about their debt without them having a physiological or even physical reaction. The fear that has been created fuels an industry. Oh yeah, it's all about the money. Think about it.

If you're fearful of "bad" credit, you're an ideal customer for (1) credit card counseling, (2) credit monitoring programs, (3) financial coaching, (4) special credit card offers, (5) credit restoration systems and the list goes on and on.

Now, I'm not advocating that you go out and explode your credit card limits. In fact, that's the last thing I recommend but what I do encourage you to do is to realize that there is a wise and an unwise way to use credit. As a budding Millionaire Manifesto you will want to have credit available to you should you need it.

You can't enjoy the fruits of your labor if you're a serial mismanager of your credit cards. The key is balance. Some people institute boundaries to keep them on track. I am one of those people. I carry a debit card and an American Express.

In other words, it's either cash or cash for me. Since the American Express bill has to be paid at once it acts as a second debit card. This has worked for me. Credit cards are seductive, they are not bad. They are, at the core, good. It's the misuse of credit cards that causes the pain and suffering of so many people. So, change the energy you have around credit cards and see them for what they are - excellent tools when used properly.

I am an intentional millionaire.

The Wealth Playbook

7 Inpowermentals™ That Will Accelerate Your Millions

First of all, what's an InPowermental™?

I coined this word in 2004. As I said in an earlier passage, I don't believe I can empower anyone but I do believe that one of my God-given gifts is in helping people to find and access the power within them – in-powerment.

Throughout my basketball career one of the words my teammates and I came to love and hate hearing from coaches was that we were going to work on the "fundamentals" in practice. That always meant it was going to be a boring practice where we did nothing but a bunch of drills to develop our foundational skills. Yuck! So, inpowermentals are the fundamentals of inpowerment. That's where the word came from. But unlike basketball practice, these 'mentals are fun!

Launching With Intention

Before you begin on this new journey toward financial transformation, please take a moment to clarify your intentions. Are you ready to proceed with conviction and apply yourself with purpose? You've taken a giant step in the right direction but are you committed to complete the journey with 100% dedication?

I want you to see yourself in this "new" light. Now I want you to write what the "new" you looks like. How the new you carries him or herself. How does the new you respond to potentially stressful situations? How does the new you talk about money and success? How does the new you incorporate spiritual principles into your pursuit of money, happiness or success?

Change the way you see money and the vision for
your
life will be transformed.

As we move into the Wealth Playbook portion of the book,
I want you to start by writing your statement of intention.

_____

_____

_____

_____

FINANCIAL FREEDOM UNPLUGGED

To have a better shot at getting what you want, it's a good idea to know what you want. Financial freedom means different things to different people. What does it mean to you? How do you define it?

I will be financially free when I...

_____

_____

_____

_____

_____

_____

Look at your definition. Is it aligned with your purpose? Is it in line with your highest good? Before we can get into the inpowermentals, let's be sure we're not falling prey to some of the biggest money predators in existence. The following phrases ring through corridors all across the world. Take a moment to think about these deterrents and how they – or similar beliefs – can be working against your quest for financial freedom.

Deterrents to Financial Freedom

Most dangerous phrase: *I already know that*

Here's the deal. We come to this world equipped with everything we need to become everything that we desire.

Yes, that includes the capacity for extreme intelligence. Intelligence is good but know-it-all-ness will stop you dead in your tracks.

Part of being an intentional millionaire has to do with surrendering your ego. Giving up this incessant need to create a persona that you are all-knowing. If you are willing to grow, willing to be open to learning some new concepts or twists on some old ones, you'll see accelerated growth not only in your financial life but in all areas of your life.

Replacement Declaration: I am open to learning new things and concepts. I am open to growing in all areas of my life.

Most dangerous habit: *Apathy*

Only talking about being financially free will never make it a reality. In fact, it'll just frustrate you and the people around you. Apathy is nothing but a lack of real interest or motivation to do something. You've taken the step to buy a book on manifesting, now it's time to take another step in the direction of that desire.

Replacement Habit: Do one thing each day to move you closer to financial freedom. This can be something as simple as reading the financial section of the newspaper. It can be clipping coupons. It can be saving $5 this week. Just do something!

Most dangerous thought: *I'll never be financially free*

Here's the real deal. We all have a finite amount of time on this planet. We can spend it productively or passively. Saying that you'll never be financially free is the battle cry of victims! You create your reality. Your thoughts create as you speak. So, every time you speak that kind of reality, you create that kind of reality.

Replacement Thought: I am financially free in this moment. I am a good steward of my finances.

Most dangerous habit: *Not paying yourself first*

If you get into the habit of doling out your earnings before you put something away for you, you'll have a very difficult time manifesting financial freedom. Remember, the Universe is abundant. There is enough for you to meet your obligations, take care of your family, give back to your community and contribute to your spiritual community if you so desire. There is more than enough!

Replacement Habit: Sock something away for you every day of the next 30 days. Even if it's a nickel. Every day put something away for you. You will be amazed at what happens for you. Don't judge what you put away. It's all GOOD!

Most dangerous belief: *I'm not worthy*

What you believe becomes life-like. There is nothing you can do to become worthy of riches and do you know why? Because you were <u>born</u> worthy! That means that the earth's abundance is yours if you choose to receive it.

Replacement Belief: I am worthy. God has ordained my riches.

Inpowermental™ #1:

Get In The Spirit

The subtitle of this book was chosen carefully. Winning The Wealth Game With Spirit. I wanted to make it clear that I believe that we must lead with Spirit. We must be guided by something greater than ourselves. If you'll look at the wealthiest people in the world, 90% of them are guided by a desire, a higher calling to do something good for the world. This leads me to an important part of being an intentional millionaire.

Soul Essentials vs. Ego Desires

I believe that every soul has a divine assignment. We were all created with a purpose. Some of us discover that purpose, step into it and live it joyfully. Some of us never quite figure out where we belong. For those of us who are clear about our soul's purpose, life is one adventure after another.

There's a distinct difference when you're living out what is essential for your soul's existence versus what your ego, your personality, desires. The ego desires the biggest car on the block so that everyone can talk about you at the neighborhood meetings. The soul knows that the big car is simply an extension of God's blessings. In other words, by being one with your soul's purpose on the planet, you will undoubtedly attract tremendous abundance. This financial prosperity might lead you to buy the biggest, fanciest car on the market but in this instance you buy the car because it is perfectly in line with the laws of abundance to reward yourself for a job well done. See the difference?

When I talk about Getting Into The Spirit, I'm really suggesting that you lead with Spirit. That you be guided at all times by a desire to live in your highest good and to serve the world as you explode your income.

The Spirit of Money

There's been a lot of debate about the spiritual nature of money. I am a firm believer that the Universe is vast and that since God created everything in and on earth as "good", that money is included in that number. I'm going to coin a phrase from the Bible in the passage on "The Lord's Prayer" where it says 'on earth as it is in Heaven'. This is a perfect analogy for abundance and financial prosperity. *Below as it is above.* Heaven is described metaphorically as a place of milk and honey and streets of gold. These are all metaphors for abundance on earth.

Physical = Spiritual

You are a physical manifestation of all that is non-physical. In other words, what has manifested in the physical plane started in the spiritual dimension. Now, said another way, everything that has shown up in your life, you created on the spiritual – the invisible energy – plane first! Therefore, if you wish to see something different in the <u>physical</u> realm, you must create something different spiritually. How powerful is that?

I don't know if you saw the movie "What The Bleep Do We Know?" but I highly recommend it. It expounds on the previous paragraph to infinitum and does an excellent job of explaining what happens in the invisible world of energy and quantum physics. Rent the movie and be prepared to be amazed.

This is a perfect time to see what you're currently creating on the spiritual level. Here's a quick exercise.

Your Spiritual Currency

Rank yourself from 1 to 5 with the following statements and substitute your preferred name for God.
1 – Strongly Disagree, 10 – Strongly Agree

____ Money and spirituality don't mix

____Getting rich goes against my faith or spiritual beliefs

____God doesn't want me to be wealthy

___I give a percentage of my earnings to my spiritual community because my minister/leader says I should

___I give more than 10% to my church because I feel guilty for having so much

___I believe preachers/leaders of churches should not accept salary

___I don't think tithing or giving to my spiritual community is needed

___I'd rather give my money to charity rather than my church

___If I don't give money to my church, God isn't happy with me

___God doesn't care if I give money to the church

___My spiritual health affects my ability to attract prosperity

___If I get too much money, I'll attract greedy people

___I'll become less spiritual if I get too excited about making money

___God withholds money from us to teach us lessons

___I can't truly love God if I desire money

___If I don't desire money, God will bless me in other ways

___I believe I'm more spiritual than people with money

___It's wrong to want to be a millionaire

Look back on your answers and ask yourself this question?

Are my spiritual beliefs getting in the way of manifesting my millions? Remember, everything physical started spiritual. So, the reality that's staring you square in the face was created by your spiritual energy first.

One final thing. We tend not to believe anything that's beyond our five senses. If we can't see it, smell it, taste it, hear it or touch it, some of us think that it's not real. But I suspect that you bought this book for the <u>promise</u> of what could happen to and for you as a result of reading it. Am I right? That's faith. Take the energy that you created when you pulled out your credit card or cash to buy this book and direct it inward. That same faith energy is what you need to attract your millions. It's not <u>all</u> you need but it's certainly a good place to start. Let's continue to the next inpowermental.

Inpowermental™ #2

Choose New Thoughts

New Thoughts, New Results

Intention precedes thought. That's why Inpowermental #1 was about spiritual harmony. Now, let's get into the nitty gritties of creating wealth.

Every thought creates something spiritual or physical. Right now as you read this book you are creating thoughts. They are either thoughts that serve your highest good or they're thoughts that go against your highest good. Either way you are choosing your thoughts in this very moment. Most people don't realize it but they do indeed choose their thoughts—they don't just happen.

But how can that be, you ask? Thoughts happen so quickly. Yes, they do. That's why you must align your thoughts with your intention on a momentary basis.

How many things do you do each day? Think about it. You shower, bathe, brush your teeth, eat, sleep, laugh (I hope) and talk. On a daily basis you do all of those things. I want you to add "aligning your intention with your thoughts" to your list. I'm not talking about praying or meditating. Those are things that are typically "outer directed" activities. I'm talking about doing something that is completely inner-directed.

Here's one way to do this. Your intention is the currency of your highest good. It desires not only what is best for you but also what is best IN you. I want you to sit quietly, close your eyes and breathe. Breathe in your highest good.

Breathe in all that is real and perfect and whole. This is your intention. Now, for clarification, perfect in the spiritual world is not an ego-defined term. It has nothing to do with accurateness and correctness. Perfect means complete. So, breathe in your completeness. Breathe in love. Breathe in light. Breathe out everything that is not those things. How beautiful is that? You're going to breathe in the things that are closest to Spirit and let everything else fall away. You are now in a place to align your thoughts with your intention. In fact, that's exactly what we just did.

Repeat this exercise at least once a day. Make it a part of your life and you will start to see mind-boggling results immediately.

What Are You Worth?

Earlier in the book I asked you to close your eyes and see what you were worth. Then I asked you to imagine someone bringing that amount of money to you. I asked you to envision receiving what you were worth. I had you do that exercise for a couple of reasons. First, receiving is an important part of manifesting millions. Second, one of the reasons many people fail to prosper has to do feelings of unworthiness. Feeling that they don't deserve such abundance.

Here's a powerful anecdote that you should read at least 10 times.

You will only attract what you believe you deserve.

One day about three years ago at one of my trainings I asked seminar participants to write one number on a sheet of paper. How much they were worth a month. One by one people held up papers with numbers as low as $1,000 to numbers as high as $1,000,000.

I approached one seminar participant who had scratched out about five different numbers before coming up with one he could live with.

"Are you worth $25,000 a month?" I asked.

He answered, "I think so."

But that wasn't what I'd asked. "Are you worth $25,000 a month?" He repeated his answer.

"I think so."

I said to this man, "Until you can say and know within your soul that you are worth $25,000 a month, you will never see $25,000 a month."

A year passed and I saw the same man at a professional function. "How's business?" I asked. "It's going good," he replied. "I'm making about 12,000 a month." He seemed thrilled.

"Great," I replied. "Is that what you're worth?"

"Yes," he answered quickly.

"Then that's why you make $12,000 a month."

He looked shocked. The weight of those words fell hard on his shoulders. He'd finally gotten it. I started to head into the ballroom for the rest of the workshop when he called out my name.

"Wait!" he said with a huge smile on his face. "I get it."

"Good," I said.

The next time I saw this man, he was making over

"$25,000 a month."
Moral of the story? Know your worth.

Here's A Thought
If you ever want to know just how generous the Universe is, drive down one of the busiest streets in the town where you live and ask yourself, "How do all of these businesses stay in business?" The answer is simple. The Universe is generous. That means that there is plenty of money for us all to be actualized millionaires. The Universe supports what is necessary. That's why there are million-dollar success stories happening every day!

As You Thinketh...
This week I want you to choose one day that you're going to write down as many of your thoughts as possible. If you can't write them down, record them into a mini disc player or tape recorder. Every thought.

Here's what's going to happen. You are going to become so acutely aware of your thoughts that you are going to find yourself wanting to "choose" better thoughts. That's good. That's the whole point. Program yourself to choose positive, affirming thoughts and once the programming is in place, it will become automatic. This is exactly how your current way of thinking came to be!

Abundant Thinking

Start to think abundantly. What does that mean? Think expansion. Not just where your finances are concerned but in all areas of your life. Love more. Give more of yourself to your relationships. Laugh more. Smile more. Understand more. More, more, more. Once your thoughts are conditioned for abundance, you'll attract more abundance.

When you expand your thinking, you expand what is possible for your life. If you have only a little, it is because you are holding space for "littleness".

There's a fish in Japan called a Koi. If you put a Koi into a fish bowl it will grow to a size that is agreeable to that size bowl. If you put it in a large tank, it will grow to the size of that tank. You are like the Koi fish. If you are still swimming in a gallon sized tank that is the degree to which you will expand. If you want more abundance, enlarge your tank! This process starts by enlarging your vision.

Inpowermental™ #3

Harmonize Your Finances

Getting Real Financially

In the next section I want to give you some tools to support you on your journey to becoming an Intentional Millionaire. The first of these is an exercise on personal financial statements. Everyone needs to know where they are financially. The reason most people don't know where they stand financially is because they don't want to know. They don't want to face the music. The unknown is feared. Today, we're going to face the unknown and trust me, you'll survive. You'll do better than survive. Armed with this knowledge, you'll thrive. Guarantee it.

Personal Financial Statements

To know where you want to be, know where you are...

Take out a sheet of paper, grab a pencil and fill in the worksheet on the next page. Next to each line place the appropriate amount. You're basically creating a worksheet that reveals your current financial scenario.

YOUR PERSONAL FINANCIAL STATEMENT

Assets

Cash in checking

Cash in savings

Real Estate Owned

Vehicles Owned

Stocks, Bonds, etc.

Life Insurance (cash surrender)

Personal Assets

Liabilities

Mortgage

Vehicle Loans

Credit Card

Real Estate Notes

Personal Debts

Retirement, IRA, etc.

Assets – Liabilities = Net Worth

SAMPLE PERSONAL FINANCIAL STATEMENT

Assets

Cash in checking	$10,000
Cash in savings	3,000
Retirement, IRAs, etc.	75,000
Real Estate Owned	125,000
Vehicles Owned	12,000
Stocks, Bonds, etc.	100,000
Life Insurance (cash surrender)	20,000
Personal Assets (jewelry, antiques)	10,000
TOTAL ASSETS	**$355,000**

Liabilities

Mortgage	$45,000
Vehicle Loans	14,000
Credit Card	6,500
Student Loans	4,000
Personal Debts	1,500
TOTAL LIABILITIES	**$71,000**

NET WORTH	**$284,000**

This is a simplified worksheet. A financial statement can be pretty extensive but for the purpose of you having a clear snapshot of where you are today, this example is sufficient. Take a look at the figure on the right side of the equal sign. Is that number in the black or in the red? In other words, do you have a positive or negative worth?

Hold that thought for a second. I want to do another quick exercise before you get stuck on that figure. That number is not the most important number in your life. It's merely one of the figures you need to be aware of as you become an actualized millionaire.

BEFORE WE GO ON...

The number on the right side of the net worth equation is only one expression of your financial net worth, however, it has absolutely nothing to do with your SELF-WORTH!

LIFETIME EARNINGS QUESTIONNAIRE

How much money have you made in your working lifetime? Write the number below or in your journal.

Lifetime Earnings

Can you imagine making that amount in one year? How about in one month? What about one week? A day? It's possible, ya know. There are people who make your annual income in one day. If they can do it, so can you.

Your game plan for bringing more prosperity into your life will be unlike anyone else's. So keep that in mind as you go through the rest of this book. Focus on becoming more aligned with your authentic self and you will begin to attract more things, more people, more circumstances that are more in line with you and your purpose.

MONEY TALKS

If I called you on the phone right now and asked you how much money you earn annually, what would be your first response?

    a) "It's none of your business."

    b) "Why do you need to know that?'

    c) "I don't discuss money."

    d) I don't have any issues sharing the
       information

If your response was close to a, b or c, I want you to get in touch with that emotion. Why is the subject of money taboo with you? Write the answer below.

_____

_____

_____

_____

Now, let's be clear. I am NOT interested in how much money you make. I am interested in what you're feeling right now about the question, though. The answer to that question is important to your development as an intentional millionaire. If you have any discomfort with revealing your income ask yourself why? But don't just ask yourself the question, answer the question on a heart level.

ASSIGNMENT

Over the next 7 days I want you to talk to a friend, spouse or family member about the question on the previous page. You'll discover more insights into your emotions around money. Record what you learn about yourself.

Money Messages Exercise

In the past, I've felt like I should have been more

_____ with my

money because

_____

I used to feel _____ when I wanted to buy

something and I didn't have the money because

_____

_____.

My current financial picture could be improved by taking

the following steps.

_____

_____

_____.

_____Yes, I'm committed to taking these steps beginning today.

The Money Message Exercise is critical to your growth because it's important to access the messages we've sent ourselves where money is concerned. We can change those messages and consequently change their effects on our future behaviors.

MONEY TRAUMA

Even the things we THINK don't affect us have a funny way of dominating our lives. One on my millionaire coaching clients once said, "My mom spent money like it was going out of style so I made sure I did just the opposite."

This person became a Squeakers profile, holding on to her money so tightly that she stayed in the same income bracket for over 5 years. Why? Because her energy around money became so constrictive that it didn't feel like it would survive in greater amounts! In other words, the subconscious message this woman sent to her money was that 'she had all the money she needed and she didn't want any more because she didn't want to become her mother'.

What money trauma have you allowed to dominate your life? Think about a situation in your past that's still present. Have you failed to attract abundance because of this trauma? If so, what steps can you take today to lay a fresh foundation to allow your money to grow?

_____

_____

_____

_____.

_____ Yes! I am making the commitment today!

Rich Kid, Poor Kid

When I was just out of college, working my first "real" job, I met a young woman who had just manifested her first million. She'd had a rather rough upbringing. Her father, a doctor, had died when she was in elementary school and her family was forced to downgrade their lifestyle significantly. Her mother had a difficult time making the transition from upper class to middle class and ultimately to the point that they had to seek public assistance. She was devastated.

My friend decided that she was going to become rich if it killed her because she desperately wanted to help her family. She got involved in a network marketing company and made a million dollars within two years. She was barely 25 years old. She made good on her promise to take care of her mother but a funny thing happened after she made all of that money. She couldn't shake the effects of having lived in public housing. She couldn't get rid of her "poverty" mindset.

So, although she now had money, she was so afraid of losing it that she couldn't enjoy it. And because her greatest fear was that she'd lose it all and have to go back on public assistance, she worked herself to the brink of death. It wasn't until she was lying in a hospital bed and I was holding her hand, did she acknowledge that her "money demons" had gotten the best of her.

That day she vowed to work on developing a healthier relationship with money. Today, she has manifested millions upon millions of dollars and the best part is that she's doing so in a balanced, spiritual manner. She's a new woman.

Your Millionaire Mentality

Find something in your current financial reality that you'd like to change. How will changing your mindset from one of limits and lack to one of prosperity, change the complexion of your situation? Jot it down...

RANDOM RELATED-UNRELATED EXERCISE

Five things you'd do tomorrow if you had more money...and how doing it would make you FEEL

Example: If I had more money, I'd buy a home for one of the families affected by Katrina. This would make me feel **helpful.**

1.

2.

3.

4.

5.

Inpowermental™ #4

F.I.T.E!

You've Gotta Have F.I.T.E.

There are four things that will turbo charge your ability to bring about financial expansion. This simple acronym is a powerful component of my Millionaire system. I believe that it takes FITE to achieve anything worth having.

FOCUS
INTENTION
TIME
EFFORT

If you want to truly understand why you are <u>where</u> you are in your life in any area, check yourself out in these four areas. I don't care if it's career, money, love, family, whatever. If you are not blissful in any area of your life, check to see how much focus, intention, time and/or effort you've put into it.

FOCUS

Focus is nothing more than putting a substantial amount of energy toward something. See, most of us really do want to be actualized millionaires but only a few of us are willing to focus on bringing that kind of abundance into our lives.

When I started playing basketball, I realized early on that I wasn't going to be the fastest player on the team. I wasn't going to be the strongest player on the team – that just wasn't my body type. With the help of my brother, Alonzo, I discovered the power of a niche. I was going to be a great shooter. That was going to be my focus.

So, on the weekend, we'd go to the gym and we'd shoot jump shots for hours. By the time my high school season started I was one of the best shooters on the squad even though the girls on the team had been playing since they were 5 years old. I, on the other hand, hadn't started playing organized hoops until that year – at age 15.

Would I have become the best shooter on our team without that focus? Never.

Which area of your financial life needs your focus today? Do you need to set up a savings account? Do you need to pay yourself first? Do you need to cut down on entertainment expenses and transfer those monies to an investment account? Take a moment to set a few action steps in the area of focus. Start today.

INTENTION

Over the last year I've spent more time with actualized millionaires than I ever have in my life and if there's one thing that unites these millionaires from those who have yet to manifest riches, it's that they are purposeful people. Self-made millionaires don't accidentally become Millionaire Manifestos. They intend to become Millionaire Manifestos.

Take my friend Farrah Gray, an actualized millionaire by the age of 15. Farrah decided at age 6 that he wanted to drastically change the complexion of his family's life. His journey from public assistance to Wall Street is well documented in his book, Reallionaire: 9 Steps To Becoming Rich From The Inside Out. In it, Farrah shares the pain of seeing his mother work from sun up to sun down. After her second heart attack Farrah made a vow. One day he was going to make enough money so that his mother would never have to work again unless she chose to.

Farrah had always loved to cook so he began mixing syrups in his kitchen. One day he came up with a tasty combination - strawberries and vanilla. He attended a huge food show in Chicago and within a short period of time, his concoction was bought by an international company for $1.5 million dollars. He was 15 years old. For Farrah, success was sweet but being able to contribute to his family was even sweeter. Now, at 21, Farrah continues to build his empire through his involvement in real estate, media, fashion and philanthropy. He's truly an intentional millionaire.

TIME

You can focus on bringing more money and prosperity into your life, you can meditate or pray all day long but if you don't put in the time, you won't make a dime. Just not gonna happen. One of the things that you will become keenly aware of on this journey is that while I encourage you to surrender to the spirituality in all things, it's also essential that you DO SOMETHING!

In September 2005, I started an innovative business and wealth coaching program called The 100 Women Millionaires Challenge. The program duration was 12 weeks and to launch it, I hosted a series of free teleconferences to allow people to find out about the program and to become more acquainted with me.

On the first call there were over 75 women on the line from all over the world. I explained some of the details in the curriculum and then at the end of the call, I revealed the tuition, which at the time was only $1,195. Eleven hundred dollars to be mentored and coached to actualize your millions. A small investment for a potentially enormous payday, right? A six-figure program being offered for less than 10% of the cost! I was certain people would jump all over it. I thought, "I'll have to close registration and turn people away."

That night, I made a special offer. I took an additional $200 off the price of the tuition, bringing it to $995 for the 12-week program. That's less than $100 a week. I was sure this added incentive and price reduction would remove any and all barriers to signing up for the program. That night, one entrepreneur took advantage of the special offer. One.

There were three additional weeks of free teleconferences. Three more weeks to be in an environment that was all about helping these women realize their dreams of entrepreneurship and financial freedom.

The next week 50 women showed up for the call. About half of the previous week's attendance. I wasn't surprised. Here's why. The majority of the people in the world let their finances dictate their actions. When these women heard "$1,195", they hung up the phone metaphorically. Trust me, I understand. I used to have a similar consciousness.

I'd get all excited about something until I saw the price tag and then I'd be like a deflated balloon. "Oh, poor me, it's just not in my budget right now" or the favorite standby phrase of the highly terrified, "It's just not meant to be." Bologney!

Before I became an actualized millionaire I'd let money stand in the way of doing something that I knew would catapult me to the next level. Some of you reading this right now are allowing a few hundred dollars to keep you from a lifetime of financial freedom. But if we continue to bail on our dreams because we "perceive" that we can't afford to finance them, we'll never become actualized millionaires. Never!

The time it takes to manifest millions is no more than it takes to work your 9 to 5. Since I started using the principles in the intentional millionaire system, I have actually worked less, vacationed more and made more money. I made more money in the last three months than I made last year alone. Am I any smarter than I was last year? Sure, a little but here's what's changed.

I've become more intentional. I've stopped making excuses. I've stopped being chicken. And best of all, I'm open to all that God has in store for me. Before I only wanted a fraction of those blessings. Not too much.

How many of you have uttered one of these phrases?
- I don't need a whole lot.
- I don't want to be too rich!
- It doesn't take a whole lot for me to live on.
- I'd be happy with just a portion of Oprah's money!

Well, guess what? That's all you're going to get. Pick your poison, my friends. You are setting the stage for a lifetime of mediocrity if your thinking's aligned with any of the above statements. The Universe is abundant. Receive joyfully.

EFFORT

The principles in the Intentional Millionaire system are for those who want accelerated prosperity, make no mistake about it. Buying this book was effort. Reading this book requires even greater effort. Implementing the principles in this book requires even more effort than reading it but you're doing it, right? You're making the effort.

In 1996, the year the NBA announced plans to support the launch of a women's professional basketball league, I was thrilled. After all, it had been my dream to play ball on American soil since college. The chance to play in front of my friends and family again was especially exciting. There was just one issue: I hadn't played competitive basketball in over seven years!

When I looked into getting into the league I discovered that most of the teams had already "preselected" their players and to make the odds tougher, only a few teams were having open tryouts. One of those teams was the Houston Comets. I was living in Austin at the time and thought, boy, how awesome would it be to play in Texas where I'd gone to college and where my family still lived?

So, I started making some phone calls. Everywhere I turned doors were being shut in my face. Finally, I decided that it was in my destiny to play in the inaugural season of the WNBA. I set my intention to play that next summer and subsequently started to train.

Shortly after I became intentional about it, an opportunity arose to play professionally in Switzerland. So, I packed up my gear and headed to Zurich. If all went well I'd be back in the States in time for tryouts with the Houston Comets.

Now, remember, no one had invited me to tryouts – I was simply staying the course and making the necessary effort for when the time came to try out. In the Spring of 1997 I returned to the Texas after a great season in Switzerland. I telephoned the new coach of the Comets' organization, landed a tryout along with about 200 other women – and yes, subsequently made the team and became a part of history by being a member of the Comets' first WNBA championship team in 1997.

Would this story have had such a seemingly miraculous ending had I not instituted every single element of the F.I.T.E. system? It's doubtful that I could have achieved this incredible feat without focus, intention, time and effort. In fact, I'd go as far as to say that it would have been impossible. Now it's your turn to put F.I.T.E. to work for you.

FITE Exercise

I can increase my cash flow in the next 30 days by FOCUSING on...

I can decrease my expenses by becoming more INTENTIONAL in the following area(s)...

I am committed to putting in more TIME in the area of _____ because doing so will

_____

_____

By increasing my EFFORT in the following areas

_____

I will see immediate results in

_____

_____

Inpowermental™ #5

Clear The Clutter

Clutter and crowdedness promotes stagnation. Energy – and money <u>is</u> energy – cannot flow in a stagnant environment

Your job in the next 24 hours is to unclutter your life, particularly the places where your money lives.

TOOLS NEEDED:

- Digital Camera
- Paper clips
- Bank Statements
- Checkbook
- Wallet
- Purse

HOW IT WORKS

Within 15 minutes you will become acutely aware of what I mean when I talk about your money being able to breathe. We are about to unclutter your money canal so that more of it can flow into your life. Now, this is only one piece of the puzzle. There's also all of that emotional and psychological stuff that we did in Part I of the book. It all works together for the good of your money.

Let's get cracking. Take out your wallet, your purse, your money clip, wherever you keep your money. Take it out and follow these instructions.

Step 1: Take an actual, or if you don't have a camera, a visual snapshot of how you are currently handling your money. If you've got receipts mixed in with the money or money stashed in five different compartments, take a picture of each different section.

Step 2: Organize all the bills, coins, receipts, etc. into their separate stacks

Step 3: Make sure all of the bills are facing the same direction. Gather all of the coins in one place. Quarters with quarters. Dimes with dimes. Nickels with nickels. Pennies with pennies.

Step 4: Put your receipts in a folder or file where you'll deal with them for taxes later. For now, we're focusing on your money.

Step 5: Bless your money. Place the bills and coins front and center. Now repeat these words: *I am grateful for you, what you are today and what you will become tomorrow. I respect you. I appreciate you. I realize that you are an extension of my energy, my spirit, my being. Therefore I bless and honor you today and always.*

Finally, over the next 10 days take note of how you handle your money. Keep it organized. Keep it uncluttered. Keep a journal. Continue for the next 10 days. And another 10 days until it is in your natural rhythm to be organized financially.

The Prosperity Matrix

This next tool helps me attract more than just money. It is a constant reminder that spirituality is at the center of every area of my life. Nothing happens without a spiritual

connection and everything, I believe, should be
approached from a spiritual angle.

Prosperity Matrix™

Emotional	6-month target	Financial
30-day target	Spiritual	60-day service target
Mental	90-day check-in	Physical/Health

EMOTIONAL

The upper left box of the Matrix is Emotional because I believe that the journey of an intentional millionaire begins with our hearts. It'll take a great deal of heart to address some of the issues in Part One of the book. Your imprints, conditioning and beliefs. It'll take even more heart to embrace the fact that you were born a millionaire and now all you have to do is step into that truth and let the cash flow!

NEW EMOTIONS

Which emotion would you like to feel around your money? Think back to the emotions list in Part One of the book. Which emotions have been dominant when you thought or talked about money in the past? Now, replace that emotion with a healthier, more positive emotional goal.

Make a wealth declaration.

When I think about money or discuss money, I feel

_____

_____

6-MONTH WEALTH TARGET

This is the date you will have achieved a major financial goal. Which area of your financial scenario deserves your immediate attention? It could be to clean up one entry on your credit file. It could be to pay down your mortgage. It could be to refinance your student loan. It could be to save $10!

Whatever you choose be sure you can succeed. In other words, don't set a completely unrealistic goal because if you fall short of it, it's only going to feed that little gremlin inside of all of us that tells us that we can't do something great. So, make your 6-month goal a baby step that's more of a stepping-stone to your long-term goal, okay?

What's your 6-month target?

_____

_____

FINANCIAL

The financial box represents your ultimate goal. Your wildest dream. Write that figure into this square.

Write it. Your wildest financial dream. What is it?

_____

_____

30-DAY MONEY TARGET

This is a baby step that you can and will achieve in the next 30 days. Your pick. Make it financial in nature. Make it something that you can monitor on a daily basis.

What's your 30-day target?

SPIRITUAL

This is your commitment to commune with your Source. To inhale all good things and exhale all that is not authentically you, therefore, authentically God.

What will your daily communion look like?

_____

_____

60-DAY SERVICE TARGET

This is your commitment to use at least a portion of your wealth to serve the world. Find a cause that's near to your heart and start sending energy to that cause until you can start sending money. Name your cause and make a commitment to it today.

MENTAL

What do you need to do to stay in the money game mentally? Read books, listen to audio, download money tips, subscribe to money newsletters or count your money? It's up to you. Remember, it takes the right mindset to create riches. Feed your mind food that will nourish prosperity and richness of mind, body and bank account.

90-DAY CHECK-IN

Okay, so it's been 3 months since you read the book. At the 90-day mark it's time to do a quick check-in with yourself. Use ICTABAH as your tool. You'll be checking these categories:

Imprints: Which old imprints are still at work in my life?

Conditioning: Which conditioning is helping or hurting my chances of actualizing my millions?

Thoughts: Are my thoughts aligned with what I want to create?

Attitudes: What are my new money attitudes?

Beliefs: How are my beliefs changing each day?

Actions: What am I doing differently that is moving me in the direction of manifesting riches?

Habits: Which new habits am I forming that are healthy?

PHYSICAL/HEALTH

Without your brain and your physical body it's impossible to manifest your empire. So, this box is on the Matrix to remind you that it's not all about the money. To be able to enjoy the fruits of your labor you must TAKE CARE OF YOURSELF. Make a commitment to nurture your mind and body each day.

What's your commitment to your health?

_____

_____

BRIINGING THE MATRIX ALIVE

Here's my recommendation. Make several copies of the Prosperity Matrix. Place one in your office, one in your wallet or organizer, another in your car and a final copy in a prominent place at home. Why these four places? There are 24 hours in a day. Here's how most of us spend those 24 hours.

Work/Job/Office	9 to 15 hours
Meal hours	2 to 3 hours
Awake hours at home	4 hours
Sleeping hours	5 to 7 hours
Getting ready for work	2 hours
Travel to and from work	2 to 3 hours

By having a visual memento in the four places that you spend the most time, you'll have a constant reminder of your goals and millionaire mission.

Daily Affirmation

Today I declare that everything I need to become more of who I already am is within me.
I release this powerful declaration into the universe, peacefully having faith that what I intend for my life, is already happening.

Inpowermental™ #6

Practice Wealth Health

Boot Camp Essentials

You are an athlete. A superstar in the game of wealth building. Therefore, you must train like a champion athlete. In every game there are several elements. You must be sure that your Wealth Health Program integrates the following components.

Coaching

The year Tiger Woods fired his coach, he stunk up the greens. It's a well-known fact that we all achieve more when we have a mentor and/or coach pushing us to become our best or our highest self. You need a wealth coach. Make a commitment to work with one in the next 30 days.

The sooner you can start to recondition yourself under the guidance of someone who can challenge you to become more, the better results you'll achieve. There's a wonderful Chinese proverb that says, "To know the road ahead, ask those coming back."

Self-directed conditioning

The Intentional Millionaire contains everything you need to build wealth. Your charge is to figure out which areas require your immediate attention. Throughout the book I've given you tools and exercises to draw that information out of you. The critical next step is for you to define your specific action steps and then begin to take action. Self-directed conditioning is practice in the world of champion athletes.

It's like an athlete in the off-season. You have to put in the time each day to work on your specific development areas. If you know that you need to work on limiting belief systems, use the tools in this book to replace old thoughts and beliefs with new ones. If you know that freeing yourself from old imprints is the biggest challenge for you, that's where you need to focus your intention.

Practice, Practice, Practice

Every day is a winding road, as one popular song says. And every day offers you the chance to move closer to financial freedom. Use everyday occurrences to elevate your skills as a money manager.

Pay attention to everything that happens because it's all connected. Remember, what's happening with you financially is connected to what's happening emotionally, spiritually, physically and mentally. Don't compartmentalize your money issues but instead, seek answers by examining the realities in all areas of your life.

Wealth Training

How do Venus and Serena, Lance Armstrong and Tiger Woods stay at the top of their games? By being exposed to the best training. For Wealth Champions the training comes in the form of books, seminars, CDs, retreats and constant education. Your commitment to a life of wealth must incorporate a variety of vehicles to help you succeed - and stay on top of the game. A good place to find all kinds of educational tools at prices you'll like is **www.half.com**.

Rewards

The time is always right to applaud your efforts. Reward yourself appropriately when you hit a milestone. Even if it's what you might consider a baby milestone, celebrate it just the same! Recognize your growth and your efforts every day. If you're keeping a journal, have a page that is full of nothing but PRAISE for you!

Rest

Wealth building is work but it should be FUN too! Be sure you're taking time to smell the coffee or roses or whatever you enjoy smelling.

Inpowermentals™ of Wealth

Make a copy of these declarations and say them daily.

$ I create my financial reality

$ I enjoy managing my money

$ I appreciate the money I have

$ I attract money

$ **My money attracts money**

$ My passive income supports my lifestyle

$ **I am financially free**

$ I work by choice

$ **My money allows me to be of greater service**

$ My wealth <u>adds</u> to my happiness, it doesn't define it

$ **My self-worth has nothing to do with my financial net worth**

$ Prosperity, abundance and wealth are extensions of my spiritual well-being

Inpowermental™ #7

Create Multiple Streams of Income

The Road Less Traveled

There are essentially three ways to become an actualized millionaire. Inheritance. Investments. Ingenuity. Of course, there's also the lottery but that won't be covered in this book. All three methods are viable, I suppose, however, one stands out in my mind as the easiest and most effective way to become a Millionaire Manifesto within the next year and that's ingenuity. In-genius. The genius-in-you. That's it!

With that being the focus on the final Inpowermental, here are the three most important kinds of income that I'm recommending that you focus on as you go forth and actualize your millions.

Active – you or someone connected to you engages in the day-to-day business operation. This could be your entrepreneurial venture that's netting you a cool million.

Passive – you are engaged in the business but not on the day-to-day level. People who own parking lots, vending machines, coin-operated businesses or even real estate, are passive income earners. They earn money in some cases without lifting a finger.

Residual – you may have been involved in the business at one time or you could still be involved but basically money's deposited into your account based on your previous efforts. Network marketers are a great example of residual income earners. So are book authors, musicians and other individuals who earn royalties for their intellectual properties.

Right now I want you to stop reading this book and take a look around you. Within two feet of you are multiple million-dollar ideas that someone had once upon a time. Some of them are earning millions actively, some are earning millions passively and some have moved on to other million dollar ideas and are simply earning residuals.

Think about it. The chair you're sitting in. The shoes on your feet. The clothes on your back. The place where you live. The book you're reading is making someone a millionaire in this moment. My printer runs a multi-million dollar business. The company that shipped your book is a multi-billion dollar company. All of these multi-million dollar business enterprises started with what? An idea. Genius? Absolutely!

So, that's the focus for the next few pages. How can you take your own genius and spin it into an empire? Here are some ideas. The next million dollar idea could be yours by taking one of the following seven steps...

STEP 1: Introduce a new product.

Pretty self-explanatory but the key is to create a product in an arena that has high demand. Apple revolutionized the portable MP3 player industry with their introduction of the IPOD.

STEP 2: Compete in existing million-dollar product

Netflix and Blockbuster duke it out in the Home DVD delivery world and both are laughing all the way to the bank. There's room for competition!

STEP 3: Find a niche product that's hot

Who would have ever thought that Doggy Day Care Centers would become such a hot business? Someone took what appeared to be a simple concept and turned it into a national phenomenon.

STEP 4: Blaze a trail with a new invention

Start writing down every time you're faced with a problem and you can't find a professional to provide solutions. These are fertile grounds for million-dollar ideas and inventions. This is how the microwave was born!

STEP 5: Extend an existing product or service

Kinko's is a prime example of product and service proliferation. They started out as a copying service company and is now an international business solutions company providing everything from copying to printing to imaging services.

STEP 6: Improve an existing product or service

How do you think we got squeeze bottle mustard, ketchup, toothpaste and lotion? Take a look around at something you're passionate about and see how you can improve it or make it more attractive to a specific market.

STEP 7: Joint-venture with an existing product or service

This is a big one. If you're in an arena that already has a solid following, there's a chance you can approach the business owner about a joint venture deal. The gym I used to belong to developed JV deals with chiropractors, massage therapists, nutritionists and acupuncturists to offer a wide array of services to their fitness clients. The professionals either paid a percentage of their business revenues to the gym or they rented the space to do business. Either way, both parties won.

Creating Multiple Streams of Income

I asked this question earlier in the book and now I'll ask again. If you had to create $10,000 income ethically and legally within the next 30 days, how would you do it? If your life depended on it, how would you go about bringing those funds into physical reality?

Write down 10 strategies you personally could implement to start generating cash flow in the next 30 days.

_____

_____

_____

_____

_____

_____

_____

_____

189

_____

_____

If I told you that you were only allowed to generate this income using your brain, the computer and the phone, what would you do? List 10 additional strategies.

_____

_____

_____

_____

_____

_____

_____

_____

_____

_____

Did the list change? Are there repeat entries? Here's what I'm getting at. As an Intentional Millionaire you need to begin to "think" and "act" like the millionaire you are. Millionaire Manifestos may share many qualities but the single thread that runs through every single Manifesto is that they all have MULTIPLE STREAMS OF INCOME.

So, forget the people who balk or laugh at the fact that you have your hands in several pies. That's good! Forget those skeptics who still believe the old school mantra "jack of all trades, master of none". People who think that's true are broke! Don't buy into that thinking.

So am I saying that you should spread yourself thinner than a sheet of notebook paper? Nope! I'm saying that in order to secure your financial freedom you will need to be involved in at least 3 different streams of income. You may only start with one but the word of the day is PROLIFERATION.

You can take one area of expertise and spin it into an empire. I produced a home study course entitled "How To

Turn Your Expertise Into A Multimedia Empire". It includes over $10,000 worth of information that people can use to turn their ideas, their genius into an empire by becoming syndicated columnists, radio or TV hosts, authors, audiopreneurs and much more. The entire course is about leveraging nothing but your brilliance. It's not about developing a prototype for a product – which is great – but I am living proof that you can take one idea and turn it into a billion dollar enterprise.

Take The Intentional Millionaire system as an example. It's already a book and seminar series. I've recorded a pilot for a radio show and I probably won't stop until it's in some form for television. All from one idea.

Here are a few outstanding examples of brand proliferation:

Chicken Soup For The Soul – books across more than 50 different consumer demographics. 100+ Million sold.

Martha Stewart – TV's domestic goddess has two syndicated television shows, a magazine, a line of kitchenware and a production company.

Oprah Winfrey – TV's Queen of Daytime has her own film and television studio, a successful talk show and magazine.

PDiddy – He started as a rapper then became a producer. Now his hip clothing line, Sean John, is setting fashion records.

Donald Trump – What else is there to say about The Donald? He is the King of Multiple Streams of Income. Real Estate. Several companies. And lets not forget his hot reality show, The Apprentice.

Rachel Ray – Can someone who admits that she's really not a good baker become TV's most likely foodie? You may know her from her Food Network TV shows *Cooking with Rachel Ray* or *30 Minute Meals* but now this perky foodologist also has her own syndicated talk show, a flagship magazine and most notably, the blessings and mentorship of O (yes, Oprah)!

WHERE WILL YOUR NEXT MILLION COME FROM?

Take your own expertise or passion. Could you spin it into a multimedia empire? Of course you can. Write an area of expertise (or passion or interest) in this blank.

_____

Next, place a check beside all of the ways you could proliferate this idea, expertise or passion.

____Ebook	____ Seminars	____Audio
____Speaking	____Video	____ Infomercial
____Coaching	____Training	____ Teleseminars
____ Website	____Licensing	____Film
____Books	____Royalties	____Affiliates
____Corporate	____Courses	____Consulting
____Consumer product		____ Company

Now that you have a sense of where you "could" take your ideas, let's develop an initial action plan. Yes, initial because I believe action plans should be fluid. They should evolve.

Action Plan

Take a look at the check marks in the exercise on the previous page. It's time to make some commitments. Remember, the journey to a thousand miles starts with one step. You're going to monitor your progress along this journey so there's plenty of time to adjust and make changes.

Here are the five things you need to get in place.
Knowledge, Market, Plan, Coach.

KNOWLEDGE

Do you have the knowledge you need to open for business tomorrow? If not, what do you need to do to gain additional knowledge?

RESEARCH

WHERE CAN YOU GET THE KNOWLEDGE?

I am making a commitment to increase my knowledge in
the areas of

TARGET DATE FOR COMPLETION:

MARKET

Is there a market for the empire I want to build? Which
companies are currently meeting the needs of this market?

I am making a commitment to find out the latest
developments in my industry.

TARGET DATE FOR COMPLETION:

PLAN

Have you already done a business plan for this enterprise? If not, here are the areas you need to consider before you open shop.

Business Overview – what business are you going into?

Industry Size – How large is the potential customer base?

Competitors – Who's doing what you want to do?

Market – Describe the customers you'll serve.

Capital Needs – How much money do you need to get started and run for one year?

Contingency Plans – How will you stay in business if you build it and they (customers) DON'T come?

COACH

Everyone needs one. Find a coach in your business area or close to it and become an apprentice. Even if you have to do your apprenticeship over the phone or Internet, you'll gain valuable experience by working with someone who understands where you want to go and who can help you get there.

TARGET DATE TO FIND A COACH: 30 Days

Closing Ceremonies

You've taken the first step toward transforming your life. I hope you feel inspired by what you learned on the Intentional Millionaire journey. My goal was to challenge you to find out more about you and your relationship with money so that you can create a life of tremendous wealth in all areas of your life.

Money is so vital to our everyday existence yet few of us ever truly understand our spiritual connection to it. I've learned so much on my own money journey that I simply had to share it. I trust you will do the same with the wisdom you've gained. Share it. Pass it on. Encourage everyone you meet to manifest their millions. It's thrilling to know that inside of all of us is the capacity to be rich beyond our imagination.

The challenge is bringing this wonderful truth into physical existence. Shortly before she died actress Beah Richards said, "The world we want to live in, we have to create." I want to help create 100 actualized millionaires each year left on my life contract. I believe this is a realistic and worthy endeavor. What could be more rewarding than helping people realize their potential? I can't think of many things.

Finally, I have some pretty ambitious goals for this year. One is that I speak in front of one million people over the next 12 months. Another goal is to have The Intentional Millionaire read by 1 million people over the next 18 months. Both of those goals should keep me busy for quite a while.

What about you? What commitments are you making to yourself and the world around you? Remember, it's not just about what you can achieve, it's about how much your contributions and achievements can change the world.

I'm ready to continue on the journey, are you?

To Your Empire!

Fran Harris

Special Gift For You

Congratulations! By purchasing this book, you and one guest are invited to spend the weekend with Fran at one of her Millionaire Spirit Boot Camps – free of charge. That's a $3,595 value!

This offer is valid until December 31, 2006 and is made only on a first come, first serve, and first seated basis. To reserve your spot, go immediately to www.intentionalmillionaire.com.

At the boot camp you'll have an opportunity to grow and learn in an electric environment with other people who are creating lives full of abundance and wealth. Whether you're financially comfortable, living paycheck-to-paycheck or so broke you can't pay attention, you will discover ways to attract unimaginable prosperity through the techniques Fran teaches in this intimate and dynamic environment.

So, register today at www.intentionalmillionaire.com and let the transformation begin!

Recommended Resources

INPOWER UNIVERSITY

Millionaire Spirit Boot Camp – 3 days

This high-octane weekend will rock your world and change your financial forecast forever. You'll learn how to apply spiritual principles to achieve your financial goals. Plus, you'll leave inspired and equipped to actualize as a millionaire or billionaire.

Intentional Millionaire Teleseminars

The principles taught in the Millionaire Spirit Boot Camps are taught in teleclasses several times a month. For details go to www.intentionalmillionaire.com.

Women Entrepreneurs & Millionaires Challenge - Teleclass

A multi-week wealth and business coaching program that's done 100% over the phone and via the Internet. Targeted to women, moms and anyone in between.

Speaker's Boot Camp – 3 Days

Earn money by sharing your passion, expertise and experiences. Learn how to select the right topics, get rich in your niche, market yourself, set fees and build an empire through informational products.

Train The Trainer Certification 3- Days

Earn a six-figure income by leveraging your expertise. The training business is wide open for energetic, confident and competent educators. Learn how to design your workshops, deliver them in the most engaging fashion and clean up in back of the room sales. Learn secrets of million dollar earners.

10 Minutes 'Til Air – 3 Days

There are over 700 different television channels, over 1,000 radio stations and over 200 Internet radio outlets, which means that the need for content, personalities and expertise is on the incline. There's a chance that you could be hosting your own podcast, radio or television show within the next 30 days. This seminar shows you how to find the right idea, pitch to the appropriate buyer, produce and syndicate your own show, secure advertisers and make tons of money!

Coach The Coach™ Certification

A WNBA Champion, NCAA Champion and Olympic team alternate, Fran has a unique perspective on human achievement. Her one-of-a-kind coaching philosophies and accelerated learning techniques will fast track your coaching practice.

BOOK FRAN FOR YOUR EVENT

Fran Harris has been called one of the most dynamic communicators in the world. Her heart-centered, humorous, engaging and content-driven presentations are legendary. To find out how you can bring Fran to your organization, send an email to **info@franharris.com** or call 310.590.7191 today.

NEW PRODUCT RELEASE!!!

How To Turn Your Expertise Into A Multimedia Empire

In this powerful, content-rich course, author, speaker, infopreneur and national TV personality Fran Harris provides over $10,000 worth of coaching, expertise and information to help you build your own multimedia empire.

She takes you step-by-step through the process of developing and launching a multimedia empire.

Includes...

A 200-page home study course packed with tips, shortcuts and insider information that will save you hours of time in research while exploding your income!

Plus! A wide array of multimedia files that you can use to model your own radio show, talk show, podcast or short form TV series. Fran takes out all of the mystery. All you have to do is step into your multimedia mogul mode and let the magic begin!

Order Today!
www.franharris.com
310.590.7191

WE WANT TO HEAR FROM YOU!

If you enjoyed The Intentional Millionaire, we invite you to email us a quick testimonial to use in our marketing materials.

Send comments to info@franharris.com

THANKS!

The Intentional Millionaire